# Delaware Lights

# Delaware Lights

## A History of Lighthouses in the First State

BOB TRAPANI JR.

Charleston History London
PRESS

Published by The History Press
Charleston, SC 29403
www.historypress.net

*Cover image*: Harbor of Refuge Light is routinely pounded by the Atlantic Ocean.
*Photo by Herb Von Goerres.*

First published 2007

Manufactured in the United Kingdom

ISBN 978.1.59629.021.1

Trapani, Bob.
 Delaware lights : a history of lighthouses in the First State / Bob
Trapani Jr.
    p. cm.
 Includes bibliographical references.
 ISBN-13: 978-1-59629-021-1 (alk. paper)
 1. Lighthouses--Delaware--History. I. Title.
 VK1024.D35T74 2006
 387.1'5509771--dc22
                          2006034631

This book is dedicated to my lovely Ann-Marie and our three children,
Nina, Katrina and Dominic.

# Contents

# Contents

# Acknowledgements

The creation of any book is a team effort; therefore, I would like to extend a very special thanks to the following individuals: U.S. Coast Guard Chief Michael Baroco, Hazel Brittingham, James Claflin, U.S. Coast Guard Master Chief Dennis Dever, E. Michael DiPaolo, Stephen Jones, Scott T. Price, John F. Sarro, Harry Spencer and Ann-Marie Trapani.

I would also like to sincerely thank the following individuals and organizations: *Cape Gazette*; Sandy Clunies; Penny Czerwinski; Jeremy D'Entremont; Delaware Public Archives; Delaware River & Bay Authority; Delaware River & Bay Lighthouse Foundation; Delaware State Historic Preservation Office; Dr. William Duncan; Dennis Forney; Gail Fuller; Lewes Historical Society; Robert J. Lewis; Ernie Mabrey; Maritime Exchange for the Delaware River and Bay; Russ McCabe; Sherry Mitchell; Pilots' Association for the Bay and River Delaware; Judith Roales; United States Coast Guard Aids to Navigation Team Cape May, New Jersey; United States Coast Guard Aids to Navigation Team Philadelphia, Pennsylvania; United States Coast Guard Historian's Office; Trish Vernon; Herb Von Goerres; Warren Walls; and last but not least, the Good Lord—the Divine author of life itself.

# Introduction

Few other man-made structures stir the emotions and imaginations of people quite like a lighthouse. Their majestic presence along America's vast coastlines and inland waterways speaks volumes for our nation's humanitarian spirit, prosperity and engineering prowess, while their very history parallels that of the United States. Our country's economic growth, military might, scientific advances and the benevolent spirit that was extended to an untold number of immigrants seeking a new life in America, all have a deep-rooted connection to lighthouses.

For the state of Delaware—the First State in the Union—lighthouses have shone a bright light on its rich history, beginning with the establishment of the legendary Cape Henlopen Lighthouse in 1767. Delaware lightkeepers under the United States Lighthouse Service and later the United States Coast Guard, were steadfast in their duties to "keep a good light" no matter the conditions. From enduring epic storms and harrowing winter ice floes to severe isolation and monotony, the keepers of Delaware lighthouses and their families forged a lasting legacy that has left an indelible mark on the lives of past, present and future Delawareans.

It is my hope that this volume will not only educate readers on the history of the First State's lighthouse heritage, but that it will also inspire people to become actively involved in present-day efforts to save and preserve these stately guardians of the sea.

Automation and technology may have rendered the keepers of yesteryear unnecessary, but in many ways the keepers have never left our lighthouses. Today the "keepers of the lights" remain in the form of the volunteers, whose passionate and dedicated efforts as lighthouse preservationists are helping to save Delaware's lighthouses and their history for future generations. As you read the historical accounts within the pages of this book, it is my hope you too will be inspired by the lure of the lights and become a "keeper" of Delaware lighthouses.

# Chapter 1

## Cape Henlopen Light Station
## 1767

There was no other lighthouse more intricately woven within the history of Delaware than the venerable Cape Henlopen Lighthouse. Completed in 1767, the granite sentinel's piercing bright light helped guide colonists to the doorstep of safety and prosperity even before the birth of America and its independence from England in the wake of the Revolutionary War.

The light's looming presence over the moving sands of Cape Henlopen was such a comfort to mariners seeking the entrance to Delaware Bay from the Atlantic Ocean that many considered the inanimate object a friend, and for good reason. An observer in the late 1700s noted, "The wrecks which lie plentifully scattered over the beach afford a melancholy proof of the necessity of a lighthouse to the approaching navigator."

The effort to establish a much needed permanent light at Cape Henlopen came from the urging of port merchants of Philadelphia in 1761, who sought to protect their valuable cargoes and ships from the dangers associated with entering Delaware Bay. The December 31, 1761 edition of the *Pennsylvania Journal and Weekly Advertizer* printed an advertisement announcing the creation of a ten-thousand-ticket lottery for the purpose of raising funds to build a lighthouse on Cape Henlopen. Roughly nine months later, on September 5, 1762, Pennsylvania proprietors Thomas and Richard Penn granted two hundred acres of land in Sussex County to the General Assembly of Pennsylvania in order to accommodate the construction of a lighthouse.

Workers began to clear the landscape and construct the lighthouse during the spring of 1764 on a site located about one-quarter mile back from the destructive reaches of the Atlantic Ocean. Apparently the construction of

Cape Henlopen Lighthouse. *U.S. Coast Guard photo.*

the lighthouse progressed far enough along in 1765 to establish a temporary light atop the structure since colonial records cite the expense of oil for Cape Henlopen Lighthouse.

According to *The History of Cape Henlopen Lighthouse, 1764–1926* by Douglas J. Evans, "As there was no sand hill there at the time, the lighthouse was built on the largest hill that could be found in the pines. The trees were cleared away and the foundation was dug. The lighthouse was built in the form of an octagon tower, eighty-seven feet tall and one hundred and thirty feet above sea level." Evans went on to note, "The walls were made of rock and each wall was seven feet thick at the base and four feet thick at the top. The interior was made of wood with a landing every thirty feet. The keeper's house was built fifty yards from the light, a small stream separating the tower from the house. The grounds surrounding the buildings were covered with beautiful grass and large pine trees."

Since the state of Pennsylvania held the deed to Cape Henlopen Lighthouse, the Philadelphia Board of Wardens was given the responsibility of making repairs to the light station. When the lighthouse was first built, whale oil was used as the fuel for the light source. Later, due to the scarcity and excessive cost of whale oil, the lightkeepers used lard and mineral oil to produce the flame for the beacon's system of eighteen lamps and reflectors.

# Cape Henlopen Light Station, 1767

At one point during the Revolutionary War in April 1777, the British man-of-war *Roebuck* and another sloop-of-war anchored just off the lighthouse. Legend has it that British soldiers rowed ashore and asked the lightkeeper for some cattle grazing nearby to resupply their ships with meat. Upon hearing their request, keeper Hedgecock reportedly informed the soldiers, "I'll give you no cows, but if you don't get out I'll give you some bullets!" Though the soldiers left at that time, they later returned with even more personnel and allegedly destroyed the lighting system atop the lighthouse, in addition to burning the tower's interior wooden staircase.

The *Roebuck*'s ship logs do not mention this incident, which is quite strange since action of this kind would have been noted by the commanding officer aboard the vessel. There is a belief that the keeper's own carelessness in knocking over a lamp and spilling lamp fuel about the lantern is what may have caused the interior to be consumed by fire. In any event, the lighthouse remained darkened for the remainder of the Revolutionary War until it was finally relit in 1784.

As history reveals, the altering effects caused by erosion at Cape Henlopen would exact a heavy toll on the light station site. The sculpting winds blowing across the cape powered a phenomenon of moving granules that defied all forms of counter resistance dating as far back as 1788 when the Philadelphia Board of Wardens first noticed the adverse impact of the cape's shifting sands. After viewing the altered state of the cape where just a few years ago it had looked noticeably different, the Wardens noted, "Every precaution should therefore be taken to secure the foundation from the growing effect of this evil."

On August 7, 1789, responsibility for lighthouses was transferred from the individual colonial states to the federal government through the Ninth Act of Congress when President George Washington signed a bill entitled "An Act for the Support of Lighthouses, Beacons, Buoys, and Public Piers." The Philadelphia Board of Wardens and the State of Pennsylvania officially ceded Cape Henlopen Lighthouse to the federal government on September 28, 1789. The newly created federal lighthouse service assumed various names throughout its history. To eliminate confusion, I will simply refer to the organization as the United States Lighthouse Service (USLHS).

A lighthouse was only as effective as its light, and in an effort to upgrade America's beacons, the USLHS began to refit the nation's lighthouses with the highly effective French-made Fresnel lenses. In 1855 the Cape Henlopen Lighthouse received a first-order classical lens, thus transforming a mediocre light source into a brilliant beam that cast its light seaward twenty-plus nautical miles.

The 1858 *Light List* notes the Cape Henlopen Lighthouse was located on the south side of the entrance to Delaware Bay and showed a fixed white light 180 feet above sea level. The tower itself was described as being painted white with a black lantern, standing 69 feet in height from the structure's base to the light's focal plane.

Though the lighthouse received a first-order Fresnel lens twenty years earlier, the 1875 *Annual Report* makes note that the tower's existing lantern was reducing the light's maximum effectiveness. According to the report, "The lantern is of the old style, and obscures a large quantity of light. It is the only one of this kind in the district. The light being a very important one, a lantern of the most modern construction should be supplied. An appropriation of $8,000 is asked for that purpose." Despite the vital importance of this seacoast light to navigation thirteen more years would pass before any action would be taken to remedy the situation.

Through the years, the persistent concerns stemming from the ceaseless shifting of the sandy cape continued to stalk the indomitable lighthouse. The June 5, 1890 edition of *The Herald & Torch Light* described the mysterious movement of the cape. The article, which was entitled "A Travelling Hill," noted, "'Without doubt one of the most interesting features of the Atlantic coast of the United States, and, in fact, one of the most interesting phenomena of the whole country, is the travelling hill of Cape Henlopen,' says a letter from Lewes, Delaware, to the *New York Sun*."

The newspaper went on to report, "A ridge of sand more than a mile long, fifty feet high and two hundred yards wide in the base, is rolling inland like a mighty wave from the sea, and with a power that is irresistible. Judging by what the people say here, the wave travels not far from fifty feet a year where its course is not obstructed by the forest, but even there it travels perhaps 35 or 40 feet. It has covered half-a-mile in forty years."

The Lighthouse Service once again tried to combat the alarming effects of the shifting sands in 1905 by placing several tons of brush around the base of the lighthouse, as well as the station's oil house, in an effort to prevent the foundations of each structure from being undermined by the loss of sand. The measures—though temporarily helpful—were unable to stave off the undeniable inroads being made by the elements.

The USLHS continually made Congress and the State of Delaware aware of the perilous plight overtaking Cape Henlopen Lighthouse, though no serious effort was made to protect the stalwart guardian from the grave dangers posed by the sea and the relentless shifting sands. Had the public been indifferent to the light's dire dilemma prior, a powerful winter storm on January 4, 1914, would provide a stark reminder to the tenuous existence of Delaware's beloved beacon.

# Cape Henlopen Light Station, 1767

Cape Henlopen Lighthouse was decommissioned in 1924. *U.S. Coast Guard photo.*

The January 5, 1914 edition of the *Washington Post* reported that this storm had wreaked havoc throughout Delaware and that "Cape Henlopen Lighthouse is completely surrounded by water, but seems to be in no danger." Apparently because the tower was still standing, the news report disregarded the obvious: that if the sea was indeed swirling around the light's foundation, then any reprieve from disaster would be fleeting.

In an effort to convey a sense of urgency for the plight of the lighthouse in the wake of the storm, the inspector of the Fourth Lighthouse District met with the Public Lands Commission of Delaware, which was called in session to hear the concerns. According to researcher Douglas Evans, "The inspector said that he would not be willing to undertake construction of jetties on land north of the reservation belonging to the state, unless the land was ceded to the federal government. But nothing came of this because of the start of World War I."

As for the tower itself, despite the impending doom surrounding its existence, the light's keepers continued to send out a guiding beam each night, all the while mindful of fate's diabolical hand lurking in the shadows cast about the lighthouse. The 1914 *Light List* notes that Cape Henlopen showed a fixed white light with a red sector. The candlepower of the light, which changed over from an oil wick to incandescent oil vapor in 1911, was 13,000 showing white and 4,000 showing red.

The beginning of the end for Cape Henlopen Lighthouse came in 1924 when a *Report of the Commissioner of Lighthouses* stated, "In consequence of the continued inroads of the sea upon the site of Cape Henlopen Light Station, presaging its early destruction, a temporary skeleton steel tower was built at a safe location on the sand hill and fully equipped ready for lighting should the old structure fall or become so unsafe as to endanger the lives of the keepers in continuing to maintain the present light." On the morning of October 1, 1924, the golden era of Cape Henlopen Lighthouse came to a close as its beacon was extinguished for the final time. The historic light's duties were transferred to the nearby temporary steel skeleton tower that evening, which operated automatically.

During this time, a preservation champion by the name of Everett C. Johnson, a former member of the Delaware State Legislature from 1911 to 1917 and Secretary of State under Delaware Governor John G. Townsend Jr. from 1917–21, stepped up to lead a public campaign to save Cape Henlopen Lighthouse. The effort was formalized when the Secretary of Commerce granted the newly formed Henlopen Lighthouse Preservation Commission a five-year lease of the reservation on January 1, 1925. The lease mandated that the Commission "perform such construction work thereon as necessary to protect and preserve the light tower and the site thereof from destructive action of the elements."

On March 4, 1925, Everett Johnson penned an eloquent plea to his fellow Delawareans in the *Newark Post*, urging them to support the commission's cause. Johnson stated, "'Old Henlopen' is not just a bit of sentiment of a few who feel History and Tradition but it is known in every port the world over. No building in our border is so crowded with Facts, History, and Tradition as this Tower. Old Henlopen had served so nobly and well. Have we a right to let it go without some of our effort and some our effort's return known as contribution of money."

In the end Johnson's efforts were in vain, despite the fact that he waged a spirited battle for the preservation of the lighthouse. The final moment for Cape Henlopen Lighthouse came April 13, 1926, at 12:45 p.m. on a clear sunny day with only a light breeze blowing. At that moment, the last supporting granules of sand fell from beneath

# Cape Henlopen Light Station, 1767

Cape Henlopen Lighthouse fell to its destruction on April 13, 1926. *Lewes Historical Society.*

the light's foundation, causing the tower to tragically slide down the slope to its destruction.

The May 7, 1926 edition of the *Reno Evening Gazette*, Reno, Nevada, looked back on the demise of the "Old Man of the Sea," noting, "Well, the sea has had its way, and old Henlopen Light that stood so sturdily upon its buttresses of rock and ancient timbers for a century and a half, has gone crashing into the whirlpool of the tides. It is as if an ancient warrior were laid low at last. Henlopen warred with the neighboring ocean unceasingly by night and day and cheated the old devil-sea of many a fine ship and the lives of countless sailors and their charges."

The news account went on to state, "A few months ago there was a project afoot to tow an old hulk on the shallows, load it with concrete and sink it as a barrier to save the great stone tower. While the proponents of the plan hesitated, the sea wrought its final destruction. To seamen it will be as an old and trusted friend has passed away."

Looking back, it is unfathomable how the tragic demise of Cape Henlopen Lighthouse was allowed to occur. The beacon presided over Delaware's growth and prosperity from the state's inception. Arguably, no other historic structure in Delaware possessed more of a cultural fabric and a deeper sense of public appreciation than this venerable beacon. Though Cape Henlopen Lighthouse lost its battle with the sea in part to politics and inaction, the spirit of this great beacon will be honored if we learn from its loss by acting to save Delaware's remaining lighthouses here in the twenty-first century.

As for Cape Henlopen itself, Lewes historian Hazel Brittingham sums up the cherished feelings for this bygone sentinel, stating, "Although the historic Cape Henlopen Lighthouse tumbled into the sea, it remains a landmark of memory in the coastal area. The tower seems to live on in photographs, artists' renditions, and mementos purchased and displayed by tourists and local residents alike. Visitors have been known to express surprise upon learning that the lighthouse no longer exists." May the memory of Cape Henlopen Lighthouse shine on forever more.

# Chapter 2

# Cape Henlopen Beacon Light Station 1825

The Cape Henlopen Beacon Light is often confused with the legendary Cape Henlopen Lighthouse; however, they were two distinctly different structures. From 1765 to 1825, the Cape Henlopen Lighthouse was the sole guiding light showing seaward to mariners upon the headland on the south side of Delaware Bay known as Cape Henlopen. During the early 1820s, however, the federal government began contending with the moving sands of Cape Henlopen migrating annually in a steady north-northwest direction.

When the Cape Henlopen Lighthouse was first built, the structure was only three thousand feet southward from the point of the cape. By 1825 mariners could no longer utilize the guiding light of Cape Henlopen Lighthouse to safely round the cape since the sands had extended northward more than one mile beyond the venerable sentinel.

Given the facts of the ceaseless progression of the sands and that the Cape Henlopen Lighthouse could no longer safely guide ships around the tip of the cape, maritime interests lobbied for an additional light to mark the end of the dynamic sand spit. The first Cape Henlopen Beacon Light was constructed in 1825. The tower rose to a height of forty-five feet and was built of a rubble-stone masonry. The light source in the lantern room consisted of ten fifteen-inch reflectors that displayed a light visible out to sea approximately nine miles. It appears that in an effort to save money, the Fifth Auditor of the Treasury decided against establishing a keeper's dwelling at the lighthouse site, instead tasking the lightkeeper of Cape Henlopen Lighthouse to serve as the caretaker for both lights.

No doubt the decision requiring the lone lightkeeper to tend to both lights was probably not a very popular one—especially when the refreshing breezes of fall gave way to the biting winds of winter. The distance between Cape Henlopen Lighthouse and the Cape Henlopen Beacon Light was three-quarters of a mile northward. Every day at sundown the keeper would trim and light the wicks of the eighteen reflector lamps of the main light and then walk nearly a mile one way to repeat the same series of events at the beacon light.

As exhausting of a task as this might seem, his duties hardly ended there. At midnight, he would once again leave the warm confines of his home to trim the wicks of each lamp in both lighthouses so that the rays of light would continue to shine forth through the early morning hours. At dawn, he would revisit each lighthouse to extinguish and clean the lamps. Can you imagine what it was like for the keeper to trek $1\frac{1}{2}$ miles round-trip over dark and dangerous sands in the middle of the night? This "nightly stroll" became even more precarious during winter storms, when frigid winds, blinding sleet and raging breakers surged across the cape and created a quagmire of quicksand and hazardous conditions ranging from sinkholes and driftwood to storm surge. The only light the keeper had to show him the way along his danger-ridden path was a meager hand-held lantern—if he could keep it lit.

As if the physical conditions of maintaining the lights weren't enough of a challenge for the lightkeeper, he also had to contend with the deteriorating structure of the Cape Henlopen Beacon Light itself and a lack of supplies to conduct his job properly. Evidence of this deplorable situation is found in the June 25, 1851 inspection of the lighthouse:

> *Beacon Light—For a range and harbor light. Ten 15-inch reflectors and lamps, bad; lantern miserable—stove-pipe through the side of it; lantern about $3\frac{1}{2}$ feet too high (seven panes of glass); water runs through the lantern, keeping everything in bad condition; tower of rubble-stone masonry—no repairs for two years; everything in a wretched condition; threatened with being carried away by the sand; wood-work inside, rotting and going fast; whole establishment in wretched condition, and if not repaired soon, will become unfit for use; no curtains up; keeper complains very much of not being supplied with necessary articles, to enable him to keep his light in order; paint, whitewash, &c., required; no dripping-pans to tanks; tanks not marked, except with chalk; repairs made by direction of a Mr. Middleton, last year, who gave it out for a fixed sum, and never came to see if it was properly executed; tower about forty-feet nigh, of sienite; wood-work rapidly*

*decaying inside; masonry of tower very inferior, and giving way, not worth repairing; sand encroaching on tower; board fence around it, and in bad order. The point, during heavy gales, is submerged several feet.*

The inspector sums up the situation, saying it is "impossible for one man to attend these duties alone." Rather than rebuild the "wretched" Cape Henlopen Beacon, the U.S. Lighthouse Service (USLHS) decided to invest in shoring up the dilapidated structure. In 1854 the light's inferior reflector lamp system was replaced by a fourth-order Fresnel lens. Along with the upgrade to the highly effective and expensive Fresnel lens, the single-keeper situation was rectified as well by building a modest dwelling at the site and providing for a separate keeper.

Throughout this time, the sandy spit at Cape Henlopen continued to migrate and by 1864 the arm of the cape had extended 1,200 feet beyond the beacon light. Rather than rebuild another masonry tower on the shifting sands, which were prone to being inundated by storm surge, the USLHS decided to construct a screw-pile lighthouse on the end of the cape's point. This new light was exhibited for the first time on the night of December 20, 1864.

The lighthouse incorporated a lantern atop the white keeper's dwelling and showed a fourth-order, fixed white light forty-five feet above sea level from its red lantern. Nine cast-iron screw-piles were driven six feet, nine inches into the sloping and ever shifting sands of Cape Henlopen to support the two-story dwelling. A decade later in 1875 the U.S. Lighthouse Service constructed a brick fog signal building at the site, which housed a first-class steam-siren fog signal in duplicate that sounded one six-second blast at intervals of thirty-nine seconds.

The screw-pile lighthouse was designed to survive in its tough environment, although the Atlantic Ocean would have the final say. The 1884 *Annual Report of the Lighthouse Board* provides an insight to the grave situation that threatened the Cape Henlopen Beacon, citing:

*The beach is being cut away under this station, so that at nearly every high tide the sea comes up under the house. In December, 1884, brush loads, with stone was placed around the station, which caused the sand to bank up, but in a few weeks a storm carried it all away. The plank walk, 125 feet long, was rebuilt. The fog-signal machinery was thoroughly overhauled and repaired. It is the intention of the Board to put a beacon on the south end of the Delaware Breakwater. Then the present beacon can be discontinued. The station is in good order, but cannot be considered safe, as a long violent storm might thrown down the beacon.*

The original Cape Henlopen Beacon Light. *U.S. Coast Guard photo.*

Rather than try and save the Cape Henlopen Beacon Light, the USLHS designated the Delaware Breakwater East End Lighthouse, which was under construction at the time in 1884, to assume the beacon's duties. Once the construction of the Delaware Breakwater East End Light had progressed far enough along that a temporary light could be exhibited from the site, the order was given to decommission the Cape Henlopen Beacon. The 1885 *Annual Report* records the moment, stating, "This beacon having become unsafe from the undermining of its screw-pile foundation, the light was, on October 1, 1884, discontinued, and the beacon, with the exception of the piles, was removed."

Though the light was darkened forever, the final chapter for the station wasn't quite written. Since the Delaware Breakwater East End Lighthouse was not fully completed when its temporary light was exhibited, the USLHS found it necessary to maintain the fog signal station on the cape for another month. A makeshift shanty for the keeper was erected near the fog signal building. By November 1885, the Daboll fog trumpet was finally ready for operation at the Delaware Breakwater East End Lighthouse, bringing to a close the era of the Cape Henlopen Beacon Light Station.

# Chapter 3

## Bombay Hook Light Station
## 1831

ombay Hook was the last lighthouse in Delaware Bay waters before ships navigating up the bay reached the start of the Delaware River at Liston's Point, located just north of the light's position. The Bombay Hook Light Station, built in 1831, was located approximately eight hundred feet southwest of the entrance to the Smyrna River, or Duck Creek as locals referred to it. During what might be defined as Bombay Hook's heyday as a vital aid to navigation, from 1831 through the 1870s, wooden ships often sought the protective harbor afforded by the location just offshore the lighthouse.

Before the advent of range lights on the Delaware River, ship captains would generally not attempt to navigate the treacherous and winding river above Bombay Hook Lighthouse under the cover of darkness. Instead, they would time their transit up the bay from Delaware Breakwater and hope to reach the anchorage at Bombay Hook before nightfall. The harbor was also heavily used as a stopover by sailing ships awaiting a favorable tide in order to cross the dangerous Duck Creek Flat Shoals located just above the lighthouse.

But was the 1831 Bombay Hook Lighthouse the only guiding beacon to stand sentinel at the site? Though history reveals conclusively that only one lighthouse was ever built at Bombay Hook, at least one account suggests that there may have been a previous lighthouse established at the site as far back as the late 1770s. The June 15, 1978 edition of the *Smyrna Times* contained a historical feature on the Bombay Hook Lighthouse or Smyrna River Lighthouse, as the article referred to the sentinel. According to the account, the 1831 lighthouse "replaced an early structure dating back to the American Revolutionary War. Both lighthouses were erected for the

Bombay Hook Lighthouse. *National Archives.*

purpose of guiding ships into the channel, which was cut to shorten the route of Duck Creek."

The newspaper feature alludes to the fact that during both our nation's fight for independence and the War of 1812, British ships often accessed Duck Creek, most likely in smaller boats, which carried soldiers intent on replenishing their vessels' supplies of meat and other items at the expense of Delaware farmers in the area. The account notes, "At such times the lighthouse keeper was in danger of his life, and more than once the volunteer militia went to the area to defend the house. The most notable defense occurred in 1813 when a band of volunteers was organized and sent to defend the northern section of Bombay Hook Light House. Several times the job of keeper was secured by Smyrnians who were war veterans."

Maybe some concrete evidence on the existence of this possible first lighthouse will be uncovered in the future, but what history does confirm is that Winslow Lewis, a close friend of Stephen Pleasanton who was the Fifth Auditor of the Treasury and the person in charge of the United States' lighthouse system from 1820 to 1852, built Bombay Hook Light in 1831. The lighthouse was a one-story structure with a light source consisting of ten lamps and spherical reflectors placed in a lantern above the roof of the dwelling. Evidently problems arose from the outset with the light's construction due to the fact that its height was not sufficient enough to exhibit a good light during times of thick weather.

# Bombay Hook Light Station, 1831

An 1838 inspection report by Lieutenant William D. Porter describes the situation of the inadequate light and structure: "It will be necessary to raise this house one story, to permit the light to be seen above the fall and spring fogs." Three years later, in 1841, the Lighthouse Service finally acted on the recommendation and the dwelling was enlarged by the addition of a second story, and the lantern was reestablished on top of the roof. The added height of the structure enabled the light source to be seen 47½ feet above sea level by ships coming up the bay or at anchor in the harbor area and was visible twelve nautical miles under clear conditions.

To say lightkeepers and their families were isolated at Bombay Hook would be an understatement. The lighthouse was built approximately 4½ miles above Bombay Hook Point—a vast marshland and a natural haven for wildlife and waterfowl. The nearest town was the village of Smyrna, located about eight miles upriver from the entrance at Delaware Bay. To make matters worse, lightkeeper Duncan Stewart, who tended the light from 1831 to 1854, could not even take heart in the "comforts of home." An 1851 inspection report of the lighthouse revealed the many shortcomings and discomforts of keeping a light at Bombay Hook, stating, "Lantern very dirty and want of paint. Lantern leaks very much; leaked in every part of building; tower so open that it is difficult to carry a light into the lantern room."

The living quarters within the dwelling were in no better shape, as indicated in the same report, which states, "Roof of the house very open— places a quarter of an inch between the shingles; brick-work rough; floors not tongued and grooved; rough and open in the attics; garret-rooms not plastered; wooden pillar, supporting steps, much worm-eaten; cellar in bad order—wants cementing and repairs; kitchen in cellar; oil smells badly."

The same inspection report that cited all the structural deficiencies with Bombay Hook Lighthouse also stated that it was actually the daughters of the keeper who tended the light for the eighty-nine-year-old keeper Duncan Stewart. In 1854 at ninety-two years of age, keeper Stewart passed away, and his daughter Margaret applied for the position as keeper of Bombay Hook Light. The request was granted and Margaret assumed her father's salary of $450 annually to tend the light. Ms. Stewart, along with her sister, stayed at the lighthouse until her resignation in 1862.

Following the tenure of keeper Margaret Stewart, Joseph Benson of Smyrna was appointed the next lightkeeper of Bombay Hook Lighthouse on December 22, 1862. At the time, no one could have realized that Mr. Benson would "keep a good light" for nearly half a century before passing away in the line of duty. At his appointment in 1862, Mr. Benson was a robust thirty-two years of age and physically well suited for the isolated and tough environment of lighthouse duty at Bombay Hook. By no means was he a one-man show, as his wife and eventually a total of seven children proved to be vital helpers to him around the light station.

The Bombay Hook Lighthouse received a fourth-order Fresnel lens in 1855, which no doubt was a marked improvement for navigation. The 1878 *List of Towers, Beacons, Buoys, Stakes and Other Day-Marks in the Fourth Lighthouse District* describes the Bombay Hook Lighthouse as being built of brick and sporting a whitewash color. The lantern is cited as being red in color and exhibiting a fixed white light above the keeper's dwelling.

The last good description of Bombay Hook Lighthouse was provided by a December 7, 1907 United States Lighthouse Service (USLHS) inspection report just five years before it was decommissioned. The report noted that the lighthouse was painted white with lead-colored trimmings, green shutters and a black lantern. The dwelling contained six rooms in addition to a pantry and halls. The remainder of the light station consisted of a barn and oil house—both painted white—and a red brick privy.

The report also noted the lighthouse as displaying a fixed white light emitting from a fourth-order Fresnel lens housing a fourth-order single wick. The keeper accessed the lantern atop the dwelling by means of a wooden spiral stairway that rose from the "attic to the watchroom floor." The lantern itself consisted of twelve sides and was cylindrical from the floor to the glass panes and polygonal in shape above.

By the 1900s, time and technology were leaving Bombay Hook Lighthouse behind. The combination of new range lights being established on the Delaware River that enabled ships to navigate safely at night—as opposed to having to anchor in the Bombay Hook Roads anchorage—and the fact that the channel was being dredged to allow ships to cross the Duck Creek Flats Shoals without fear of grounding helped render the Bombay Hook Lighthouse less useful to commercial shipping. Though the local watermen still valued the lighthouse, it would not prevent Bombay Hook from being extinguished forever. By 1913 the U.S. Lighthouse Service decommissioned the light and replaced its duties with the Smyrna River Range.

Following the light going dark, the USLHS tried to protect the site from vandalism by having custodians watch over the retired sentinel. The USLHS maintained ownership of the former light station for the next sixteen years until a decision was made to sell the property to the owner of the adjacent land in 1929. The ensuing years would not be kind to the aging sentinel, as periodic vandalism and the elements took their toll on the structure—especially the interior. The State of Delaware eventually purchased the land including the lighthouse to form the Woodland Beach Wildlife Area.

# Bombay Hook Light Station, 1831

It was around 1965 when Smyrna residents and others made a move to save the decaying Bombay Hook Lighthouse. The *Delaware State News* reported the following in their October 21, 1965 issue: "Lighthouse May Shine as New Tourist Stop…A hundred-year-old lighthouse at the mouth of the Smyrna River may be reconditioned as the state's newest tourist attraction. Dr. Norman Spence of the state's Fish and Game Commission suggested in the Kent Levy Court yesterday that the old building off Rt. 9 in the Woodland Beach wildlife area was 'worthy of reclamation.'"

The ambition to create a tourist attraction at the site and restore the lighthouse was never realized. Fires caused by senseless vandalism continued to plague the structure over the next decade until the former lighthouse was nothing more than a brick and concrete shell of its former glory. The end for Bombay Hook Lighthouse finally arrived in 1974 when Delaware's Division of Fish and Wildlife decided to remove the structure due to the safety hazard it presented in such a remote location.

Today, only the brick foundation of the dwelling and a nearby concrete oil house remain as vestiges of this bygone light station. In time, Mother Nature will erase the very memory of the Bombay Hook Lighthouse from the banks of the Delaware River as the light's brick and mortar remnants will one day descend to a watery tomb and vanish from the shoreline forever.

Chapter 4

# Mispillion Light Station
## 1831

The Mispillion River meanders ten miles through marshland from the Delaware Bay to Milford, Delaware. The town of Milford holds a prominent place in Delaware maritime history as an active port and shipbuilding community from the late 1700s into the early twentieth century. During this long and active era of shipbuilding along the Mispillion River, at least three lighthouses were constructed at its entrance to point the way to and from the Delaware Bay, although sketchy evidence suggests that possibly four or even five lights may actually have been established.

An interesting account in the *History of Delaware, 1609–1888* by J. Thomas Scharf touches on what appears to be the first attempt to establish a lighthouse at the mouth of the Mispillion River. Scharf's research notes that an act was passed by the Delaware legislature on January 14, 1803, authorizing the construction of a "permanent light at the mouth or entrance of Mispillion Creek, near the Delaware Bay."

What is known about this vague effort to build a lighthouse was that a man by the name of Jonas Dawson sought permission to hold a lottery in hopes of raising $3,000 for the building of a guiding beacon at the mouth of the river. The lighthouse was to be maintained by Dawson and financially supported by tariffs collected from ships entering the Mispillion based on their draft and size. The lighthouse itself was to rise thirty feet in height and be outfitted with a lantern four feet in diameter, which would house a highly polished concave tin reflector three feet in diameter. Despite the passage of the state act to build a lighthouse, it appears that the structure was either never built or its existence has been obscured by time.

Conclusive history reveals the first known Mispillion River Lighthouse was completed on October 19, 1831, and though there are very few details about the beacon, records show the light was built atop the keeper's house and that its modest optic consisted of six lamps with spherical reflectors. Seven years later, in 1838, the federal government tasked Lieutenant William D. Porter with inspecting Delaware's lighthouses. The lieutenant's findings were quite scathing as he reported that "the house [is] badly built and nearly in ruins."

What is interesting to note in his inspection report is that Lieutenant Porter must have entertained doubts as to whether the location warranted the service of a lighthouse by saying the light was "in a most dilapidated state, and if it is at all necessary to have a light at this point, that light should be a good one. I therefore respectfully suggest that the miserable building at this place may be pulled down, and one erected in its place that will answer the purpose, and at the same time be a good and substantial building."

In addition to the deplorable state of the first lighthouse, erosion was quickly devouring the site on which the beacon stood. The following year, the Fifth Auditor of the United States Treasury heeded Lieutenant Porter's recommendations and rebuilt the Mispillion Lighthouse. Whether the original lighthouse was moved farther back and modified or totally rebuilt is not known, but the second Mispillion Lighthouse structure did receive a stronger light in the form of eight lamps containing fourteen-inch reflectors that showed a fixed white light from a thirty-one-foot tower. The 1849 *Light List* comes closest to solving the mystery of whether the 1839 beacon was indeed the second lighthouse at Mispillion, stating, "Light on keeper's dwelling; removed and rebuilt in 1839."

The encroaching Delaware Bay continued to threaten the Mispillion Lighthouse, prompting the federal government to purchase additional land from Charles and Mary Elizabeth Polk and Benjamin Potter in 1843. Based on the 1849 *Light List* citation of the fact that the last time the station was rebuilt was 1839, it appears the Fifth Auditor (Stephen Pleasanton) held off on rebuilding the lighthouse during his tenure, which ended in 1852. The mystery involving a possible "third" lighthouse comes from the 1857 *Light List*, which noted that Mispillion Lighthouse exhibited a fixed white light of the fifth order from thirty-eight feet above sea level. The question lies in the change in the light's focal plane from thirty-one feet in 1839 to thirty-eight feet in 1857. The Mispillion Lighthouse received a Fresnel lens for the first time in 1855 when the beacon was listed as being last "refitted" by the federal government, but why the discrepancy in the light's focal plane remains a question that history may never reveal.

*Mispillion from S.W.*

The 1873 Mispillion Lighthouse. *National Archives.*

A November 1, 1857 Lighthouse Service report informed Congress that the lighthouse was no longer required, noting, "It is reported that the light at Mispillion, in Delaware Bay, is unnecessary even for the local interests of that vicinity. It is located at the mouth of Mispillion Creek, which has at its entrance a depth of only one-foot of water at low tides. Only a few small flat-bottomed vessels run in and out of this creek. For the general navigation of the bay this light is useless, and its discontinuance is respectfully recommended."

Two more years would pass, but in 1859, the U.S. Lighthouse Service (USLHS) finally discontinued the Mispillion Creek Lighthouse after only twenty-eight years of operation. According to lighthouse historian Jim Gowdy, "The lighthouse was sold at public auction for $136 to a Mr. Dorsey, who moved the structure to Walnut Street in Milford, some eight miles to the west. It is believed the structure no longer exists." For the next thirteen years, the mouth of the Mispillion Creek was dark, making safe passage through the entrance of the waterway a near impossible feat at night, especially during low tide.

The USLHS did not record the reason why, but whatever the driving force, a new lighthouse was established at the mouth of Mispillion Creek

# Mispillion Light Station, 1831

Mispillion Lighthouse in 2000. *Photo by Bob Trapani Jr.*

in 1873. The *Annual Report* of 1872 documents the fact that during their last session of the year, Congress appropriated $5,000 "for reestablishing the small lighthouse at this point." The new Mispillion Creek Lighthouse was first lit on June 15, 1873. The 1873 *Annual Report* noted, "The light is a fixed white light of the sixth order of the system Fresnel, and is shown from a wooden frame tower, connected with the dwelling of the keeper, both colored gray, with the exception of the lantern on the tower, which is black. The focal flame is 48 feet above the water."

Although the Mispillion Creek Lighthouse was first lit in 1873, two years would pass before the 1875 *Annual Report* mentions that remodeling efforts in the keeper's dwelling were finally completed. The report notes, "Four good rooms have been added, and a good brick cistern built." This same entry further reveals that an "old nemesis" reappeared and thus became the chief concern of the Lighthouse Service—tidal flooding and its eroding effects at the light station. The *Annual Report* recommends a course of action to combat the destructive force of the tides, saying, "This site is subject to overflow by the tide, and can only be protected by a properly constructed dike, which would cost about $4,000."

The 1878 *List of Towers, Beacons, Buoys, Stakes and Other Day-Marks in the Fourth Lighthouse District* describes the wooden frame Mispillion Lighthouse as "buff" in color. The document goes on to state that the tower was connected to the frame dwelling and the beacon's lantern was painted black. The light source continued to be a fixed white light of the sixth order.

The ferocious hurricane of October 22–24, 1878, caused heavy damage to Mispillion Lighthouse and no doubt left a permanent impression on the life of its keeper, James H. Bell. The storm began by dropping light rain on Delaware Bay the night of the twenty-second, with the force of the wind increasing during the overnight hours. By morning the maelstrom was raging out of control and was described as a "terrific gale" blowing ninety knots on the morning of the twenty-third. The storm was one of the worst ever seen on Delaware Bay, with its wind, rain and storm surge sparing nothing in its way.

The Mispillion Light Station suffered the loss of its entire livestock, which was swept away from the base of the lighthouse by the tidal surge. The 1879 and 1880 *Annual Reports* make brief mentions of having to make repairs to the light station in the wake of the October hurricane, including repairs to the dwelling's front porch.

The U.S. Lighthouse Service continued trying to stave off erosion at the lighthouse during the ensuing years, noting that in 1885 "some 60 tons of riprap were placed around the banks of the station to protect them from scour and ice." An October 1890 storm wreaked havoc at the light station, which forced the federal government to repair the protective banks and raise their height and renew the boardwalks around the site. A small kitchen was added to the dwelling in 1891.

A December 5, 1907 U.S. Lighthouse Service inspection report notes that Mispillion Lighthouse consisted of a lantern atop a dwelling that showed a fixed white light with a red sector. The lighthouse was painted white with lead-colored trim, green blinds and black lantern. The structure itself stood on a pile foundation with brick piers and contained seven rooms in addition to halls and a pantry. The remaining buildings of the light station were also constructed of wood and included a privy painted white with lead color trimmings, oil house, barn, tank house, poultry house and two storehouses.

Because the site was situated in a salt marsh subject to storm surge, boardwalks connected the lighthouse with the station's outbuildings and boat slip. The total height of the lighthouse from the ground to the vent atop the lantern was listed as fifty-two feet, with a focal plane of forty-six feet. The Mispillion Lighthouse was equipped with a sixth-order Fresnel lens illuminated by a sixth-order single flat wick. The red sector was formed by ruby glass.

Life at Mispillion Lighthouse seems to have been pretty quiet over the next five years, with the only mention coming from a 1912 *Report of the Commissioner of Lighthouses* that notes the old oil-wick light was changed to acetylene gas. The upgrade to acetylene in 1911 ended the need for a full-time keeper, with only a custodian necessary to watch over the light station. The historic lighthouse was finally decommissioned on December 29, 1929, and its light moved to the newly established sixty-seven-foot pyramidal skeleton tower. The light tower, which was originally established at Cape Henlopen in 1924 to take over the duties of the threatened Cape Henlopen Lighthouse, remained an active aid to navigation at the mouth of the Mispillion River until the 1980s.

The old lighthouse was sold at public auction in 1932 and changed owners on various occasions over the next seven decades. During this time the condition of the lighthouse started to deteriorate, becoming quite serious in the 1990s. Because the lighthouse was in private ownership, lighthouse preservationists were powerless to help the proud but decaying wooden sentinel. Inspired by a series of articles in the *Delaware State News* during March 2001, Milford resident William J. Fox called for a public meeting at the Slaughter Beach Fire Company on April 26 that same year to gauge interest in saving Mispillion Lighthouse. Fox was quoted at the meeting as saying, "It's been a symbol to a lot of us. Once you've seen it from the bay, it stays with you. So much has happened in and around that lighthouse."

Mispillion Lighthouse was struck by lightning and burned on May 2, 2002. *Photo by Bob Trapani Jr.*

A group called the Keepers of the Mispillion Light was officially organized on June 14, 2001, with Slaughter Beach resident Rebecca Craft elected as the organization's president. Under Ms. Craft's passionate leadership, the Keepers of the Mispillion Light endeared themselves to the surrounding communities who were sympathetic to the group's daunting but noble mission.

During this time the Cedar Creek Group, owned by Merritt Burke III, was successful in purchasing the historic beacon from its previous owner and indicated publicly that it would be willing to work with the Keepers of the Mispillion Light on the restoration of the venerable sentinel. The potential partnership was never to occur due to Mother Nature. On the morning of May 2, 2002, Mispillion Lighthouse was struck by lightning during a thunderstorm, which sparked a fire that consumed much of the historic tower and gutted the structure's interior before firefighters could arrive on the scene to extinguish the tragic blaze.

The Cedar Creek Group sold the charred lighthouse to anonymous private preservationists, who then hired a professional house-moving firm to disassemble the historic structure and relocate it to an undisclosed site for storage purposes in mid-June 2002.

For nearly two years the whereabouts of the Mispillion Lighthouse remained uncertain and the identity of its new owners was shrouded in secrecy until the *Cape Gazette* newspaper in Lewes shed light on the mystery. The May 7–13 [2004] edition noted that "John and Sally Freeman of Washington, D.C., and Lewes said, April 30 [2004], they will move the historic structure to a lot in Shipcarpenter Square in Lewes." Today, some of the remains of the historic Mispillion Lighthouse have been beautifully incorporated by the Freemans into a replica of the proud beacon, thus keeping its memory and many contributions to Delaware's lighthouse heritage alive.

# Chapter 5

# Port Mahon Light Station
## 1831

Over a period of 72 years, from 1831 to 1903, the federal government would have to establish five different structures at Mahon River Light Station due to the ceaseless encroachment of the Delaware Bay over the marshy area on which the lights stood watch. The light station itself was known by a variety of names that included Mahon's Ditch Lighthouse, Mahon River Lighthouse and Port Mahon Lighthouse during its 124-year tenure as an active light.

There is very little information about the first lighthouse built at Mahon River. What is known is that the sentinel—originally identified as Mahon's Ditch Lighthouse—was established on the south side of the entrance to the river. The federal government obtained a five-acre plot of marshland from the State of Delaware on January 28, 1830, and by March 31, 1831, Congress appropriated $10,000 for the construction of a lighthouse, which was built by Winslow Lewis.

By 1838—just seven years after the lighthouse was established—a detailed inspection of the lighthouse by Lieutenant William D. Porter revealed serious deficiencies with the structure. Mr. Porter stated, "Light on keeper's dwelling, burns eleven lamps with spherical reflectors. The house is badly built; the plastering has fallen in many places; built of bad materials; oil house requires repairs." Navigation information from 1839 listed the height from the base to the lantern of Mahon's Ditch Lighthouse as being only twelve feet. At some point that same year in 1839, the lighthouse was either moved or rebuilt on the same tract of land by contractor Winslow Lewis and the tower's height was raised to twenty-four feet, showing a fixed white light.

# Port Mahon Light Station, 1831

The 1875 Mahon River Lighthouse. *National Archives.*

Around 1855, the U.S. Lighthouse Service (USLHS) started listing the name of the sentinel as Mahon's River Lighthouse and it was noted that the structure was "refitted." The improvements to the 1839 structure may have included moving the lighthouse back from the encroaching reach of the tidal marsh as the latitude and longitude coordinates were different from previous official mentions.

During its refitting, the Lighthouse Service remodeled the lantern room and installed a fifth-order Fresnel lens to replace the older, far less effective reflector lamp apparatus. Following these improvements, Mahon's River Lighthouse displayed a fixed light that was visible for ten nautical miles. In addition, the official lighthouse reports noted the light was now twenty-six feet in height from the base to its focal plane and could be seen thirty feet above sea level.

In 1859 time was running out for this particular tower. The 1859 *Annual Report* of the USLHS conveyed to Congress that "Mahon's River has been condemned, and preparatory steps have been taken to rebuild it. It is deemed safe, however, for the coming winter." The site chosen for the new lighthouse would be located only a short distance west of the doomed beacon.

A new lighthouse was completed and lit on December 6, 1861. Lighthouse historian Jim Gowdy described the new beacon as "a simple but handsome two-story frame dwelling surmounted by a cupola, and resting upon wooden foundation pilings." Less than ten years later, the 1870 *Annual Report* of the Lighthouse Service documented more trouble for the Mahon's River Light. The report stated that "the abrasion of the marsh along the front of the building has been considerable. The building is on the back end of the lighthouse lot, and the location will have to be changed in a short time."

Work to construct yet another Mahon River Lighthouse began in the spring of 1875 and by October 20, 1875, the Fresnel lens inside the old lighthouse was removed and installed inside the lantern room of the new beacon. The building was described as a light on a frame tower, with a two-story dwelling attached to the tower. Both the dwelling and tower were painted buff in color, with the lantern room sporting a coat of red paint. The height of the lighthouse from the base to its focal plane was fifty-one feet, and it showed a fixed white light from a fifth-order lens. The old lighthouse structure was sold at public auction and removed from the site.

Due to its ability to serve as a guiding light to oystermen returning home to Port Mahon and its value as a lateral aid to navigation for ships in the Delaware Bay, the USLHS upgraded Mahon River Light's Fresnel lens from a fifth-order to a more powerful fourth-order in 1888. In addition, panes of ruby glass were installed at specific spots in the lantern room of the lighthouse to form a red sector for navigational purposes.

The 1894 *Annual Report* of the Lighthouse Service foretold the all too familiar scenario of impending doom for yet another sentinel at Mahon's River. The board's report to Congress stated, "The constant washing away of the bank has made it necessary to remove and rebuild the lighthouse structure four times since its first erection in 1831. The present station is now threatened with early destruction."

The most eye-opening comment gleaned from the dilemma facing Mahon's River Light in the 1894 *Annual Report* was not so much the ever present threat of erosion, but the importance—or lack thereof—that the Lighthouse Service now seemed to be placing on the beacon as a vital aid to navigation. The report further revealed that "this station is hardly of sufficient importance to justify the expense of the construction of an isolated site for its use." Recommendations instead focused on solving the need to constantly have to rebuild or relocate the lighthouse by erecting a detached wooden tower 1,500 feet north-northwest of the existing structure. The logic behind this recommendation was based on the fact that the wooden tower "could be moved if necessary."

For unexplained reasons, the USLHS abandoned the idea of building a detached wooden tower to serve as the light for Mahon River and instead decided to build a fifth and final lighthouse at the site. The 1903 *Annual Report* stated, "The new lighthouse is finished, the roof sheathed, the floors laid, the exterior painted, and interior woodwork put in place and

The 1903 Mahon River Lighthouse. *U.S. Coast Guard photo.*

finished. The keeper moved in and the lens was set up in the new lantern. The light was exhibited from the new lighthouse on June 25, 1903, for the first time." In addition, the light station sported a new barn, oil house, elevated walkways and a wharf. A new road leading to the lighthouse was also established.

The lightkeeper who had the longest tenure at Mahon's River Lighthouse was Irvin Lynch Sr. During his twenty-seven years of service at the station from 1912 to 1939, keeper Lynch raised a very large family in addition to keeping a good light. Irvin and his wife, Janie, had nine children. Aside from the hardships of winter isolation and having to cope with the fury of storms along the bay's edge, living at a lighthouse was not that different from life anywhere else. The Lynch family had three horses, one cow, one billy goat, pigs and lots of chickens. Keeper Lynch also had an old Model T Ford that the family would drive on the marsh when it was dry and hard.

By 1939, lightkeeper Irvin Lynch Sr. was forced to retire from the United States Lighthouse Service due to health reasons, at which time the decision was made to automate Mahon's River Light. Sixteen years later in 1955, the lighthouse structure itself was deemed unnecessary for the purpose of showing a light. The United States Coast Guard instead erected a white skeleton tower nearby to assume the duties of the Mahon's River Lighthouse.

Port Mahon Lighthouse left to the mercy of the elements. *Courtesy of the Delaware State Historic Preservation Office.*

Once the Coast Guard established a modern tower at the site, the lighthouse property was turned over to the United States Air Force. The site around where the 1903 structure was situated then became an offloading facility for barges discharging jet fuel that was transported via pipeline to storage tanks, and eventually to the nearby Dover Air Force Base.

Before long the historic wooden lighthouse started to show obvious signs of deterioration from neglect and vandalism. Ongoing erosion also continued to devour more and more marshland around the former light station property. A flicker of hope arose during 1976 when local citizens were successful in having the fading sentinel listed in the National Register of Historic Places.

Locals desired to see Port Mahon Lighthouse preserved and thus started to spread the voice of advocacy for the beacon's salvation. Concerned citizens hoped to turn the lighthouse into a public education and recreation facility once the goal of restoration was accomplished, but somewhere along the way, those plans never materialized. By 1982 the U.S. Air Force declared the lighthouse surplus property and looked to the General Services Administration for help in finding a new owner.

In the end, the government sold the lighthouse and property at auction to the Delaware Storage and Pipeline Company—the same firm that worked with the U.S. Air Force in providing the base with jet fuel. Two years later, on December 29, 1984, a mysterious fire engulfed the lighthouse and destroyed every vestige of the historic structure, except for the cast-iron pilings. Today, sixteen rusted cast-iron pilings stand surrounded by the reaches of the Delaware Bay and are all that remains of the once-proud Port Mahon Lighthouse.

# Chapter 6

# Christiana River Light Station
# 1835

Christiana River Light Station bears many interesting firsts: it was the first lighthouse established on the Delaware River, the first light station in America to use rosin gas as an illuminating source and the first—and quite possibly the only—lighthouse in the nation to have a centenarian serve as keeper.

The lighthouse was established in 1835 to mark the entrance to Christiana Creek (now known as Christiana River) along the Delaware River. The station was located about 26 miles below the Port of Philadelphia, Pennsylvania, and was the principal guide for ships seeking the city of Wilmington, Delaware. Situated approximately 2½ miles above the mouth of the Christiana River, Wilmington was a key port for the Atlantic seaboard as it boasted a proud shipbuilding era, as well as large manufacturing interests.

Details of the early years of the light's operation are scarce. Not long after the light was established, an 1838 inspection report submitted to Congress by Lieutenant William D. Porter noted that the lantern was located atop the keeper's dwelling with a light source that consisted of ten lamps and spherical reflectors. Apparently the contractor that built Christiana River Lighthouse did not do a stellar job because after only three years of existence, the walls of the house were noticeably crooked.

By 1841 the number of lamps used to create the beacon's light were reduced from ten to eight, with oil utilized as the illumination source. In the meantime, the United States government was seeking alternative illuminants to replace oil in lighthouses due to the rising costs of the fuel. A decision was finally made in 1844 to experiment with rosin gas as a fuel

# Christiana River Light Station, 1835

Christiana River Lighthouse. *Robert Lewis collection.*

source for lighthouses, with Christiana River Light being the first sentinel in America to implement the scientific test, which was invented by Benjamin F. Coston, U.S. Navy.

The concept called for the gas to be manufactured on site by the keeper in a detached brick building. The keeper was required to follow a strict procedure in creating the volatile mixture for maximum effectiveness of the gas as well as for his personal safety. Though the production of the gas and its subsequent use inside the lighthouse was carried out somewhat successfully in 1844, the experiment was ultimately deemed impractical and was abandoned a little over a year later.

The 1858 *Light List* notes that Christiana River Light Station showed a fixed white light from a fourth-order Fresnel lens, which appears to have been installed in 1855. The light's focal plane was 48 feet above sea level, and its beam could be seen for 11½ nautical miles.

A fascinating story in American lighthouse history occurred at Christiana River Lighthouse and was uncovered by Sandra M. Clunies, a certified genealogist and historian for the Chesapeake Chapter of the United States Lighthouse Society. In a 2005 article entitled "The Christy Mystery," Clunies notes her research of microfilmed keeper registers revealed the name of Anthony Christy, who was appointed keeper of Christiana River

Lighthouse on September 22, 1853, and was later listed as "deceased" when he was replaced on September 23, 1862.

Though official lighthouse service records did not mention ages, Clunies discovered through research of census records that keeper Christy would have been 105 years of age in 1862. This fact would have made the lightkeeper 96 years of age when he received his appointment at Christiana River Lighthouse in 1853. "Can you imagine the federal government appointing a 90-plus year-old man to active duty?" asked Clunies. "When I first spotted that item on the U.S. Coast Guard web site, I went out to find supporting evidence, as it seemed so outlandish—but indeed I did find additional documentation."

Clunies validated this amazing fact when she discovered a January 27, 1878 issue of the *New York Times* featuring an article entitled "Old Delawareans," citing the *Wilmington Republican* issue of January 25. The account noted, "We are informed that Anthony Christy, the father of our well-known and respected citizen, John V. Christy, was 105 years and 3 months old when he died in 1861 [*sic.*]. Mr. Christy was appointed light-house keeper for the light-house at the mouth of the Christiana when he was in the ninety-seventh year of age by President Pierce, and served in that capacity until his death." This intriguing story reclaimed from the obscure pages of time is truly one of the more fascinating accounts associated with our nation's lighthouse heritage.

By 1874 the Christiana River Lighthouse was sharing the parcel of land that comprised the light station with a new staging ground for government buoys. The buoy yard consisted of a 50 x 150-foot platform atop stone piers near the lighthouse. Historic photographs reveal that in addition to the lighthouse site serving as a buoy yard, caisson piers earmarked for eventual establishment in the Delaware Bay as the foundations for lighthouses were staged there as well.

Official U.S. Lighthouse Service (USLHS) reports in 1878 record that Christiana River Light was a whitewashed brick building two stories high, with a slate-colored roof and tower and a red lantern. The first floor's interior was described as being divided into two rooms, with a kitchen on one side and an oil room on the other. A hallway led to the second story of the lighthouse, which was also divided into two rooms. A stairway led to the attic and lantern where a fourth-order Fresnel lens showed a fixed white light.

The 1891 *Annual Report* notes two interesting developments at the site. Apparently the lighthouse required a good dose of renovations, since it was reported that "contract was made for extensive repairs to the keeper's dwelling." In addition, the USLHS constructed a new aid to navigation on a pier closer to the entrance to the river.

# Christiana River Light Station, 1835

Once the beacon light was built, mentions of the old lighthouse were few and far between from 1892 to 1902. Other than additional renovations to the dwelling and ongoing erosion control at the marshy site, the focus appears to have been more on ensuring the smaller light was effective and kept in good condition. One item of note can be found in the 1901 *Light List*, which records the fact that the lantern of the Christiana River Lighthouse was changed in color from red to black.

The keeper of the old lighthouse appears to have been maintaining the light at the Christiana Beacon and its fog bell in 1902 based on the year's *Annual Report*. According to the document, "The fog-bell striking machine was provided with an electric starting apparatus, consisting of a magneto mounted in the hall of the Christiana Lighthouse, and connected with the fog-bell house by a No. 10 copper wire, about 2,150 feet long, mounted on porcelain insulators placed along the railing of the elevated board walk on the jetty." The fog signal at the little beacon light was placed into service on November 23, 1901.

The end of the line for the Christiana River Lighthouse would come into sight in 1906, when Congress authorized the construction of the Bellevue Range. The Bellevue Range, which was established about one hundred yards out in the Delaware River near the entrance to the Christiana River, was lit for the first time on March 15, 1909, forcing the decommissioning of the Christiana River Lighthouse. According to historian James Gowdy, the U.S. Lighthouse Service maintained ownership of Christiana River Light despite its deactivation and used the structure to house the keeper of Bellevue Range Rear Light and his family until 1937. Two years later, in 1939, the Coast Guard reportedly razed the old lighthouse for safety purposes.

# Chapter 7

# Reedy Island Light Station
# 1839

Reedy Island Light Station has the distinction of being the second lighthouse established within the boundaries of the Delaware River when it was constructed in 1839. Located on Reedy Island, which is situated offshore on the westerly side of the shipping channel near Port Penn, the lighthouse was once a vital aid to navigation for the fledgling tri-state ports of Delaware, Pennsylvania and New Jersey.

Very little is actually known about the original brick light tower and keeper's dwelling. The best informational account of Reedy Island's first lighthouse is found in the 1877 *Description of Lighthouse Sites of the Fourth Lighthouse District*. The report stated, "The tower, which is of brick, is founded on wooden piles; it is 44 feet in height from base to coping. The diameter at base is 22 feet with solid walls 5 feet thick, and at the top it is 11 feet with walls 2 feet thick." The lighthouse contained granite steps that led to the beacon's watchroom and a covered wood frame walkway that connected the tower to the keeper's dwelling.

Official U.S. Lighthouse Service (USLHS) records reveal that in 1842 this brick tower was equipped with twelve lamps and reflectors. In 1845 Reedy Island Light Station became the second lighthouse in the country to experiment with the use of rosin gas as an illuminant source. During this time the light source consisted of fourteen lamps and reflectors, which showed a fixed white light from an approximate focal plane of fifty feet. The experiment with rosin gas lasted through at least 1849, but the practice was later abandoned when the USLHS deemed its use impractical.

The island site suffered from a long-standing erosion problem, as its soft marsh mud composition was prone to being washed away by the action

# Reedy Island Light Station, 1839

A rare view of the original 1839 lighthouse tower (without its lantern) that once served at Reedy Island Light Station. *Courtesy of Jeremy D'Entremont.*

of the tides, the wakes of passing vessels transiting up and down the river and abrasion by winter's ice floes. To help protect the light station from the inundating reach of the storm tides, the Lighthouse Service built a six-foot embankment surrounding the light station. By the mid-1850s, it was necessary to begin protecting the site further by back-filling the area around the lighthouse.

Though Reedy Island's shining white light was a major comfort to mariners transiting the river under the cover of darkness, the lighthouse was of little use during periods of fog. The U.S. Lighthouse Service not only rectified this issue in 1855 with the establishment of a fog bell on the southern tip of the island, but also greatly enhanced the light source by installing a fourth-order Fresnel in place of the reflector system. In 1857 the lighthouse was listed as showing a fixed white light of the fourth order that could be seen approximately twelve nautical miles from a focal plane of fifty-five feet. The tower itself was listed as being forty-nine feet in height from its base to the focal plane.

The 1875 *Light List* noted that Reedy Island Light Station consisted of "one brick tower, and dwelling for keepers; buildings, white; lantern red. Fog-bell struck by machinery. The light shows fixed white for one minute, followed during the next minute by five consecutive red flashes (at intervals of twelve seconds)." However, the USLHS 1875 *Annual Report* issued later that year notes that with the eventual establishment of the Liston Tree ranges on the Delaware River, the Reedy Island Lighthouse would be discontinued.

The light's decommission would come to fruition on April 2, 1877, with the lighting of the Finns Point Range on the easterly (New Jersey) side and Port Penn Range on the westerly (Delaware) side of the river. Though the light on Reedy Island was darkened because of the new ranges, the station's fog bell remained an active aid to navigation in an effort to warn vessels of the island's presence during murky weather. From April 1877 to July 1879, the station was officially known as Reedy Island Fog-Signal, since the light was no longer operational.

Though the USLHS deemed Reedy Island's light as unnecessary for navigation, Philadelphia maritime interests strongly disagreed and petitioned to have the light reestablished. The February 22, 1878 edition of the *Chester Daily Times* in Pennsylvania notes, "A petition signed by all the steamship owners and leading representatives of steamship lines at Philadelphia has been sent to Mr. Harmer, to be laid before Professor Henry, Chairman of the Light-House Board, asking the restoration of the light at Reedy Island, Delaware Bay."

The newspaper account went on to state,

> *Prompt action is urged in view of the large and constantly increasing arrival and departure of steam and sailing vessels at that port. The petition sets forth that it is of great importance to navigation in the Delaware Bay that there be sufficient lights, and this general requirement embraces the Reedy Island Light. This light, being on a point of land near the ship channel, can be seen in thick weather when the distant range lights on the shore are invisible. For want of this light, vessels are often obliged to anchor through the night, involving expense and delay. The lighthouse and the keeper are there, and the only additional cost will be the running expenses of the light, which would be inconsiderable as compared with the benefits that would accrue to commerce. The petition has been laid before Prof. Henry, who seems disposed to take the matter into favorable consideration.*

The USLHS bowed to the maritime pressure and eventually reestablished a light at Reedy Island. Rather than using the old brick light tower, the government built a new keeper's dwelling and integrated a lantern atop the structure's roof. This new lighthouse was lit for the first time on July 1, 1879. As for the old brick light tower, the USLHS made use of it by removing its upper portion, capping it with a roof and converting the structure into a fog signal building. The base of the

# Reedy Island Light Station, 1839

Reedy Island Lighthouse. *Lewes Historical Society.*

former lighthouse was remodeled into an oil room to house the light station's flammable fuels for the light source. This arrangement lasted until 1883 when the fog bell was relocated forty feet south of the old lighthouse and closer to the riverbank.

Records from 1883 reveal that Reedy Island Lighthouse showed a fifth-order flashing white light every thirty seconds from a focal plane of thirty-six feet above sea level. The remains of the old white brick tower continued to serve as a daymark for mariners on the Delaware. The characteristics of the lighthouse were changed again on November 30, 1892, from a flashing white light to a fixed beacon of the fifth order, in preparation for yet another change to come at Reedy Island Light Station.

From March 14, 1896, to May 16, 1904, the Reedy Island Lighthouse served as the front light in the short-lived Port Penn–Reedy Island Range. Though the range system was discarded after only eight years due to changes in the shipping channel, the island lighthouse remained in service. The beacon came to be known as the Old Reedy Island Lighthouse from 1904 onward, in an effort to differentiate it from the newly established Reedy Island Range established on the river's western shore to the south of the island-locked lighthouse.

A 1907 inspection report notes that Reedy Island Lighthouse was a lantern tower on a frame dwelling, outfitted with a fifth-order Fresnel lens that showed a fixed white light and fixed red sector (originally installed on October 1, 1884) from a focal plane of 32 feet above high water. The lighthouse was a wood frame structure painted white with lead-colored trimmings, green shutters and a black lantern, established on a brick pile foundation. The overall height of the lighthouse from its base to vent was 37½ feet. The light station was also equipped with a long wharf that enabled a lighthouse tender to pull alongside to resupply the light station.

In spite of its offshore location, the lighthouse was electrified in 1934 via an underwater cable, but was later permanently decommissioned in 1950. The abandoned light station suffered from vandalism and deterioration before the Coast Guard eventually razed the structure for safety reasons. Today, the light's brick foundation and other unidentifiable structural remnants scattered about the site are all that remain of Reedy Island's light station.

As for the rear tower of the short-lived Port Penn–Reedy Island Range, its roots can be traced back to 1892 when the USLHS *Annual Report* made an urgent plea to Congress to establish a new range for the protection of shipping. The report provided supporting arguments for the range, stating,

> *Urgent representations were made to the Board by the various interests concerned in the navigation of Delaware bay and river as to the need of a rear light to form a range with Reedy Island light to mark the turning point of Bakers Shoal. It was claimed that a light placed near Port Penn wharf would affect this purpose. The Board caused careful examination of the matter to be made by the officers of the Fourth Light-House District. The conclusion reached and the report made was to the effect that the proposed light is much needed. This is emphasized by the fact that a fine steamer recently grounded on Bakers Shoal under circumstance which lead to the belief that, had the proposed light been in use then, this disaster would have been prevented.*

Though the range was petitioned for in 1892, four years would pass before Congress acted. The range was finally lit for the first time on March 14, 1896. The rear light for the range was located at the north end of Congress Street in historic Port Penn. The beginning of the end for the rear light of the Port Penn–Reedy Island Range came about in 1901 when Congress authorized the Army Corps of Engineers to dredge a new thirty-foot channel in the Delaware River from Appoquinimink River to deep water above Reedy Island.

This would necessitate the establishment of new ranges to properly mark the channel. The Port Penn–Reedy Island Range was finally discontinued on May 16, 1904. Once decommissioned, the rear light was disassembled and moved just up river to serve as the rear light for the newly established Baker Range. This tower at Baker Range continues to serve mariners in the twenty-first century and is maintained by the U.S. Coast Guard Aids to Navigation Team Philadelphia.

# Chapter 8

## Delaware Breakwater West End Light Station 1849

Not many people today are aware of the fact that in addition to the existing Delaware Breakwater East End Lighthouse, the Delaware Breakwater, or inner stone wall in Lewes Harbor, was home to another beacon of the sea. In fact, this forgotten lighthouse—known as the Delaware Breakwater West End Light Station—actually preceded the east end light and stood sentinel around the midway point of the breakwater wall.

The beginnings of the Delaware Breakwater West End Lighthouse are inseparably connected to the construction of the Delaware Breakwater itself. On May 23, 1828, President John Quincy Adams approved an appropriation of $250,000 for the construction of the breakwater and one year later, in 1829, the first stones were being set in the waters of Lewes Harbor.

The construction of the breakwater occurred under the watchful eye of renowned engineer William Strickland. The project took forty years, and by 1869 the breakwater's construction had cost the United States $2,123,000 and spanned the terms of twelve presidents. When completed, William Strickland had overseen the placement of 835,000 tons of stone to build the breakwater, which stretched 2,586 feet. The original goal of 3,600 feet was not achieved. The icebreaker portion of the wall also fell short of the proposed 1,500-foot section by 99 feet. Author of *Cape Henlopen Lighthouse and Delaware Breakwater* John Beach states, "Despite these short comings it was still the second greatest structure of its kind in the world." The only breakwater that was larger at the time was located in Cherbourg, France.

# Delaware Breakwater West End Light Station, 1849

Delaware Breakwater West End Lighthouse with the Maritime Exchange building on the left. *U.S. Coast Guard photo.*

Today the Delaware Breakwater is one complete structure that extends approximately eight-tenths of a mile in length, but this was not always the case. Until 1882, a gap existed between the breakwater and the icebreaker, which ships seeking a harbor of refuge accessed during stormy weather or rough seas. To mark the access between the stone structures, a powerful beacon light was established, and a decade later a lighthouse was built.

The Delaware Breakwater proved to be a lifesaver to vessels and their crews. During the Civil War, twenty-five ships made use of the harbor each day, while as many as two hundred sailing vessels could be found behind the wall during storms. The Delaware Breakwater also provided sailing ships—both American and international—the only harbor of refuge between Sandy Hook, New Jersey, and Cape Charles, Virginia.

Navigational light lists during the tenure of Delaware Breakwater West End Light record that the first lighthouse was built in 1849, though other sources indicate that a sentinel or beacon light existed as far back as 1838. An 1838 inspection report made by Lieutenant William D. Porter after a visit to the light at Delaware Breakwater stated, "Breakwater Beacon-Light…On superintendent's dwelling; has four lamps upon a different construction from those used in our lighthouses generally, and show a more brilliant light than any that I have seen in this district. Well kept." The inspection report went on to recommend that a fog bell be established at the light station to help vessels find their way safely into the harbor during thick fog.

The fact that Lieutenant Porter was sent to inspect the light at Delaware Breakwater indicates that the federal government considered the beacon as part of the district's aids to navigation system. The reason for the "more brilliant light" over any others in the district is a bit of a mystery. Lighthouse records state that though the Fresnel lens was indeed invented by this time, the United States did not purchase or install the first French-made classical lens in an American lighthouse until 1841, when the Navesink Lighthouse in New Jersey received a first-order lens. It remains quite intriguing that Lieutenant Porter was so impressed by the brilliance of the light at Delaware Breakwater.

Though the 1838 lens type is unknown, lighthouse historian Jim Gowdy provides an explanation on the confusion surrounding the construction date of the lighthouse. Gowdy comments, "The discrepancy of the two dates, 1838 and 1849, has to do with lights being exhibited from two different structures. The light in 1838 was said to be a small light on the superintendent's dwelling, and apparently, until a proper lighthouse was built by the Lighthouse Service in 1849, some reimbursements were made to the Philadelphia Chamber of Commerce and the Philadelphia Board of Underwriters, for maintaining the light on the Delaware Breakwater."

The man in charge of overseeing the construction of the Delaware Breakwater also served as the engineer for the construction of the Delaware Breakwater West End Lighthouse in 1849. Given this fact, the lighthouse became known locally as the Strickland Light in honor of its builder, William Strickland. When completed, the lighthouse was forty-three-feet tall from its base to the focal plane and had a forty-seven-foot focal plane from sea level. The beacon showed a fixed red light varied by flashes at intervals every forty-five seconds and by 1853 was outfitted with a fog bell.

A December 20, 1850 *Letter from The Secretary of the Treasury* transmitting the report of the general superintendent of the Lighthouse Service sheds more light on the Delaware Breakwater West End Lighthouse. The report states, "This is a new stone building, with the lantern on the roof. The building is raised on stone arches, laid in mortar or cement—supposed sufficiently high to be out of danger from the sea; appears a strong building, and a fair piece of work, although somewhat leaky in the roof about the lantern."

On May 1, 1876, the Delaware Breakwater West End Lighthouse received a new fourth-order illuminating apparatus designed to increase the brilliancy of the light for the "benefit to commerce." The new optic was to show a fixed light, varied by white flashes every minute and could be seen a maximum of twelve nautical miles over the entire horizon. In addition, the station's fog bell struck at intervals of ten seconds to help warn mariners of dangers obscured by thick weather. Another aid to mariners was the color scheme of a lighthouse, which in the case of Delaware Breakwater West End Light was whitewashed brick with a black lantern.

A new chapter in the history of the Delaware Breakwater West End Lighthouse unfolded on November 1, 1881, when the U.S. Lighthouse Service created the Delaware Breakwater Range. Though much discussion and planning no doubt went into the decision to create a range at Delaware Breakwater, U.S. Lighthouse Service records do not shed much light on the thought process. The only reason cited was that the range was established to guide vessels safely into Delaware Bay. The rear light for the Delaware Breakwater Range was located on land at the end of Pilottown Road in Lewes.

The 1890 *Annual Report* of the Lighthouse Service records the fact that the great storm of September 1889 carried away the Delaware Breakwater West End Light's fog bell and machinery, including the frame tower that was designed to provide the apparatus with some protection from the elements. The report also states that the light station's outbuildings were washed away, as well as the plank walks and landing steps. Following the storm, the United States Lighthouse Service decided against replacing the fog bell at Delaware Breakwater West End Lighthouse, citing the fact that "the steam-signal at the east end of the breakwater was deemed sufficient."

As far back as 1842, Major Hartman Bache of the U.S. Navy Topographical Engineers lamented the fact that the new harbor of refuge created by the Delaware Breakwater was already too shallow for the navy's largest warships. One of the primary reasons was the gap that existed in between the breakwater and the icebreaker structures. It seems that violent tidal action caused extensive shoaling inside the safe harbor, thus reducing its ability to safeguard deeper draft vessels. It took forty years for Congress to act on Major Bache's observation, but by 1882 the federal government allocated the necessary funds to close the gap at Delaware Breakwater. The work began that same year and continued for the sixteen years before the desired goal of connecting the two stone structures was accomplished in 1898.

Though the Delaware Breakwater West End Lighthouse continued to serve as the front light in the Delaware Breakwater Range, the days of the lighthouse remaining as an active aid to navigation were numbered following the gap's closure in 1898. The light's inevitable decommissioning occurred on May 25, 1903, when the United States Lighthouse Service

The former Delaware Breakwater West End Lighthouse converted to accommodate the operations of the Maritime Exchange. *Courtesy of the Maritime Exchange.*

ordered the beacon darkened. The Delaware Breakwater Range continued to serve mariners, but the duties of the front light were transferred from the west end light to the nearby Delaware Breakwater East End Lighthouse.

This would seem to have been the end for the Delaware Breakwater West End Lighthouse, but another role related to navigation would immediately surface for the timeworn beacon. The Maritime Exchange for the Delaware River and Bay, which operated in a building next to the decommissioned lighthouse since 1875, requested and obtained permission from the U.S. Lighthouse Service to occupy the vacant structure. The Maritime Exchange utilized the old lighthouse until about 1942, when their operations were relocated to land at the tip of Cape Henlopen.

Once the Maritime Exchange removed itself all together from the former lighthouse in 1954, the historic sentinel sadly began what would be its final journey into the pages of time over the next five years. Slowly but surely, the building suffered major deterioration from being vacant, as the elements and vandals exacted their unforgiving toll from the structure.

The exact date of the light's destruction is unknown, but retired Coastguardsman and local Lewes resident Warren Walls believes the light was razed and demolished for safety reasons in 1959 or 1960. Though uncertain of the year, Mr. Walls remembers serving as the coxswain for the boat that took a Coast Guard crew out to the light for the purpose of removing the hazard presented by the badly deteriorated structure. Today, only the brick foundation remains discernable atop the breakwater—a permanent tombstone of sorts that marks the site of the lost Delaware Breakwater West End Lighthouse.

# Chapter 9

# *Fenwick Island Light Station*
# *1859*

Since the day it was first established in 1859, Fenwick Island
Lighthouse has not received the kind of attention generally bestowed
upon other seacoast lights along the Atlantic seaboard. This somewhat
mysterious lack of awareness can be attributed to a few factors, including
its remote location when it was built and the fact that its purpose was for
more general lateral seacoast navigation as opposed to serving as a guide
to an important harbor or shipping junction.

In spite of the light's unassuming reputation, the beacon performed a
much-needed service to mariners sailing along the once darkened sixty-mile
stretch from Cape Henlopen Lighthouse at the mouth of Delaware Bay
to Assateague Lighthouse in Chincoteague, Virginia. During the age of
sailing ships, the practice was to sail close enough to shore to ascertain one's
position, but not too close to place the ship in danger of grounding on the
treacherous shoals that lurked a few miles off shore.

The 1850 *Blunt's American Coast Pilot* addresses the dangerous shoals
between Cape Henlopen and Cape Henry, stating, "The coast is studded
with shoals, lying at a distance off, from 3 to 6 miles from the nearest point
of land." Upon the discovery of the notorious Fenwick Island Shoal in
1850, the maritime community began to advocate for a light to help ships
pass by this dangerous location.

The Lighthouse Service made a strong case to Congress for a lighthouse
to be established at Fenwick Island within their 1855 *Annual Report*. The
report stated,

# Fenwick Island Light Station, 1859

*A light-house in the vicinity of Fenwick Island will serve to guide vessels from the southern ports, bound into the Delaware, and also the great coasting trade with the same or a more northern destination. Fenwick's Island shoal is a very dangerous one for those, and also in some degree for the European trade of Philadelphia. It is very common for ships coming from the eastward to fall in with the coast considerably to the southward of Cape Henlopen, and in thick weather a light on Fenwick's Island would serve to ascertain their position when the Henlopen light was invisible. This latter is said to have been frequently mistaken for the double light of the Five-fathom Bank light-ship.*

On August 1, 1859, the first beam of light pierced the darkened seacoast off Fenwick Island to warn mariners of the nearby Fenwick Shoals. The lighthouse towered eighty-five feet above the beach and nearby salt marshes. It was equipped with a third-order Fresnel lens that showed a fixed white light varied by one flash every two minutes.

No lighthouse in Delaware built prior to or after Fenwick Island was constructed in a similar manner to the state's southernmost sentinel. Dorothy Pepper, a founding member of the Friends of Fenwick Island Lighthouse, once described the unique construction of the light, saying, "Probably the most unusual thing about the lighthouse is that it is actually two brick towers instead of one. The outer tower is conical—that is, it is larger at the bottom that at the top—and it slants inward slightly as it rises." Ms. Pepper went on to say, "At the bottom its brick walls are 27 inches thick. At the top the outer walls are 18 inches thick. The inner tower is cylindrical—that is, it is of the same diameter from top to bottom. The inner tower walls are 7 inches thick from top to bottom and the interior diameter of the tower is eight feet six inches."

The crown jewel of Fenwick Island Lighthouse is its gorgeous third-order Fresnel lens made of precision-cut glass prisms, which stands approximately five feet two inches tall and weighs nearly two thousand pounds with its brass assembly. During the days when the lighthouse was an active aid to navigation, its fixed white light could be seen for fifteen nautical miles and could be distinguished by a white flash every two minutes. The flash was produced by an array of three flash panels of vertical elements mounted on framework on the outside of the Fresnel lens. One revolution producing a flash every two minutes was controlled by a chariot-type revolving apparatus, consisting of eighteen bronze wheels and powered by a weight-actuated clock.

From the light station's construction in 1859 to around 1867, one lightkeeper was in charge of tending the light at Fenwick Island. At some

Fenwick Island Lighthouse. *Robert Lewis collection.*

point after 1867, an assistant lightkeeper was assigned to the station, but the Lighthouse Service did not accommodate the upgrade in staffing with additional living quarters. Rather, the head keeper and his family were asked to occupy the first level of the 1858 dwelling, while the assistant keeper and his family were assigned the second story. In 1878 the Lighthouse Service sought to change these uncomfortable living conditions by requesting Congress to appropriate $5,000 for the erection of a second keeper's dwelling. The request was fulfilled and on November 12, 1881, a second, larger keeper's dwelling was completed.

The beginning of the end for the golden era of lightkeeping at Fenwick Island occurred in October 1940, when the Coast Guard sold about three-quarters of the light station property to former Fenwick Island lightkeeper Charles L. Gray for the sum of $1,610.79. Records are inconclusive as to when the light station was actually automated, but certainly by the 1950s, the combination of electricity and technology removed the need to have a keeper maintained on-site.

Instead, the Coast Guard assigned remote lightkeepers to watch over Fenwick Island Lighthouse. This responsibility fell into the able hands of

# Fenwick Island Light Station, 1859

Fenwick Island Lighthouse. *Photo by Ann-Marie Trapani.*

Coast Guard Station Indian River, which operated out of the former 1876 United States Life-Saving Station building 1½ miles north of the Indian River Inlet.

By the late 1970s, the Coast Guard no longer needed the lifesaving powers of Fenwick Island Lighthouse for navigational purposes and thus decommissioned the stately sentinel on December 13, 1978. During this time, the Fresnel lens was removed and shipped to Governor's Island in New York. The darkened lighthouse caused quite a stir among Fenwick Island residents. Not only was their lighthouse turned off, the structure was also stripped of its crown jewel—its classic Fresnel lens. "They just closed it up and walked away," says Paul Pepper, founding president of the Friends of Fenwick Island Lighthouse. "They didn't tell anybody. When they left, they took the prisms, the wiring, everything."

The citizens of Fenwick Island did not take the news of their beloved lighthouse seemingly being tossed aside in the trash heap of history lightly. Led by Paul Pepper and Dick Carter, the combination of political support that was garnered and unbridled passion and love for the lighthouse eventually was successful in having the third-order Fresnel lens restored back inside the sentinel.

On September 21, 1981, the U.S. Coast Guard transferred ownership of the lighthouse to the State of Delaware. That same day, the State signed an agreement with the newly formed Friends of Fenwick Island Lighthouse to have the organization help care for the historic Delaware seacoast beacon. The Friends of Fenwick Island Lighthouse were able to raise approximately $15,000 shortly thereafter towards their goal of relighting the beautiful Fresnel lens atop the lighthouse. Founding president Paul Pepper fondly recalled that wonderful day, saying, "We turned the light on again on May 26, 1982 and intend if it is God's will to keep it on."

# Chapter 10

# New Castle Range Light Stations
# 1876

Lighthouses in Delaware Bay were very instrumental in helping ships avoid the dangerous shoals located in the expansive bay but they were powerless to aid ships in navigation once the waters narrowed into the Delaware River prior to the late 1870s. The river's winding and treacherous path prompted the U.S. Lighthouse Service to begin establishing a system of range lights in 1876 to enable ships to safely traverse the river at night. One such range or set of "leading lights" was erected approximately $1\frac{3}{4}$ miles below the historic town of New Castle, Delaware, and was called the New Castle Range.

When the New Castle lights were completed and lit for the first time on November 15, 1876, the range consisted of two separate lighthouses, with a keeper at each one. The shorter front light, which sat at water's edge, worked in tandem with the taller rear light located approximately a half-mile from the river directly behind the front light. Ship captains knew they were in safe water while traversing the river as they approached this range as long as the rear light appeared directly above the front light. Should the rear light appear to the left or right of the front light at anytime during this stretch of the river, the ship would adjust its course or risk grounding on the shoals.

Upon completion of the light station in November 1876, a fourth-order range lens showed a fixed white light from a second-floor bay window in a square wood-frame tower, which was elevated twenty feet above water. The *Description of the Lighthouse Sites of the Fourth Lighthouse District* described the keeper's house, stating:

*The dwelling is two stories in height, with tin roof, weather-boarded on outside and lathed plastered inside. The first story is of brick, cement-washed on outside, and is divided into four rooms, one of which is used as a kitchen, one as cellar, containing cistern of a capacity of 2,000 gallons, the others as work-room and store-room. The second story is divided into four rooms with porch on front and side, level with second floor. Outside steps lead from the porch to the ground, the entrance to the lantern room being from this porch.*

A decade later, in 1886, the Lighthouse Service was forced to make a major change to the New Castle Range Front Light in an effort to effectively safeguard shipping from shoals protruding on the eastward side of the channel. The wooden light tower was detached from the keeper's house and relocated thirty feet to the west to correct the range line and allow ships to pass farther from the shoals off Finns Point, New Jersey.

The now-detached tower was made of wood and supported by a rubble stone foundation. The total height of the structure was thirty-eight feet, not including a fancy iron finial that rose another three feet above the lantern room of the tower. The actual light source was exhibited twenty-seven feet above sea level. Although there was an entrance to the lighthouse at ground level, the keeper actually utilized an entryway on the second floor that was connected to the dwelling via an enclosed walkway. When the light was originally established, the optic was a fixed white light, but in October 1894, the characteristic was changed to fixed white for two seconds, then eclipsed for one second. The light's flash was produced by a cylindrical shade that was hoisted and dropped by a clockwork mechanism.

Though many changes occurred to the light source and tower at New Castle Range Front Light over the years, one particular event remains unexplained. The 1898 *Annual Report* of the Lighthouse Service states that "this light was temporarily discontinued on May 3, 1898." The report provides no explanation as to why this action was taken. Perhaps one of the lights with this range encountered a problem with its optic or structure, or perhaps there were changes being made in the river channel that necessitated the suspension of the range until the work was completed.

Since 1876 the New Castle Range Front Light exhibited a light from the second story of the wooden tower; however, this changed around 1923. The U.S. Lighthouse Service moved the beacon's optic from the second to the third level of the tower, which increased its focal plane to thirty-seven feet. During this decade electricity would come to the light station and subsequently eliminate the need for a lightkeeper. Though it is not known when New Castle Range Front Light was automated, lighthouse historian

# New Castle Range Light Stations, 1876

New Castle Range Front Light. *U.S. Coast Guard photo.*

New Castle Range Rear Light. *U.S. Coast Guard photo.*

Jim Gowdy estimates this occurred in the 1920s or early 1930s. Once the light was automated, a custodian took the place of a full-time keeper living at the station.

Over the ensuing years, the fact that a more economical steel tower could be established that would require far less maintenance than the deteriorating wood eventually doomed the historic riverbank sentinel. In 1964 the Coast Guard decided to tear down the wooden lighthouse and replace it with a standard steel structure, which remains in service today.

Aesthetically the rear light for the New Castle Range was the more elegant of the two lighthouses. The rear light, which was $57\frac{1}{2}$ feet in height from its base to the top of its lantern, was lit simultaneously with the front light for the first time on November 15, 1876. The lighthouse was equipped with a fourth-order range lens that exhibited a fixed white light from a focal plane of 90 feet above mean low water for ships viewing the beacon from the water.

Many people mistakenly think that lighthouses only guide ships at night, but the sentinels' lifesaving powers are not limited to just the realm of darkness. During the day, whether the sun reigns high in a blue sky or cloud cover creates a plethora of grays, a lighthouse still leads ship captains past dangers lurking in the vicinity of its presence. The color of a lighthouse and its distinctive construction style combine to convey a silent message to mariners that identifies the ships' location by the lighthouse they are seeing on the horizon. Thus, the lighthouse becomes a daymark when its light isn't necessary.

In 1901 the Lighthouse Service tried to improve the visibility of New Castle Range Rear Light by painting the lantern and front of the lantern tower a solid color of black, while the rest of the structure remained white in color. How effective this color scheme was as a daymark remains unanswered, but evidently the results were less than desired. Just two years later, the 1903 *Light List* fails to mention the black color scheme, simply describing the face of the lighthouse as white with green shutters. Mariners must have deemed the all-white façade more distinctive against the backdrop of natural greens and browns along the riverbank.

As time and technology outdistanced the utility of the historic rear light, maintaining a structure that required constant maintenance became less and less attractive to the U.S. Lighthouse Service, and later the U.S. Coast Guard. The lighthouse was automated in the 1920s and sold to private owners in the early 1950s. Over the next thirty years, the historic lighthouse slowly deteriorated from neglect and was alternately occupied and vacant during that time. At some point a small fire damaged the dwelling's roof and later the lighthouse was condemned. The owner of the historic site finally hired the Goodwill Fire Company from New Castle in November 1982 to raze the structure and eliminate the hazard the deteriorating building posed.

Today a non-descript skeleton tower stands near the site of the historic lighthouse and serves as the rear light for the New Castle Range. Both the front and rear lights are maintained by the United States Coast Guard Aids to Navigation Team Philadelphia.

# Chapter 11

# Port Penn Range Light Stations
# 1877

The Port Penn Range was first lit on April 2, 1877, and played a pivotal role in helping river pilots and ship captains safely navigate the Delaware River above Ship John Shoal Lighthouse to the south and Reedy Island to the north. The front light for this range was established about 900 feet southwest of the mouth of Augustine Creek and about 1¾ miles southwest of the village of Port Penn.

The keeper's house and the beacon for the range front light were integrated into one structure, as the lantern room rested on top of the dwelling. The light was equipped with a twenty-six-inch-diameter range lens and reflector sitting behind the lens, which displayed a fixed white light 41½ feet above sea level. The 1878 *Description of Lighthouse Sites of the Fourth Lighthouse District* stated the lighthouse "is of frame, securely bolted to stone walls, upon which it rests, the stonework being founded on piles." The report goes on to say the sentinel is "two stories in height, with oil-room and watch-room and lantern above the second story."

Though the Port Penn Range Front Light stood prominently on the west riverbanks of the Delaware, the Lighthouse Service attempted to help pilots and ship captains better identify the structure from a greater distance during the day. The 1879 *Annual Report* remarked, "The front part of the roof was painted red to make it a more conspicuous day-mark." Apparently, their efforts were not quite as effective as intended, for the very next year, an entry in the 1880 *Annual Report* states that the side of the tower that faced the Delaware River was painted "entirely red, as well as the lantern of the lighthouse." Being able to identify a range light at a greater distance on the horizon helps ships gauge mid-channel much sooner—and thus, improve

# Port Penn Range Light Stations, 1877

Port Penn Range Front Light. *Robert Lewis collection.*

the chances for a safe transit in that particular segment of the river during daylight hours.

The rear light for the Port Penn Range was an entirely different type of structure, which stood 1¾ miles behind the front light. The imposing 120-foot skeletal tower was constructed of wrought iron and painted brown in color. The beacon's focal plane was 133½ feet above mean high water on the Delaware River and showed a fixed white light. The 1901 *List of Lights and Fog Signals on the Atlantic and Gulf Coasts of the United States* notes that the lightkeeper's dwelling for the station was situated a short distance to the east of the tower, painted white, with green shutters and lead-colored trim.

By 1901 plans were being made by the Army Corps of Engineers to dredge a new channel in the vicinity of the Port Penn Range—a decision that would forever alter the future of the range. Due to the changes, the Port Penn Range no longer was able to guide ships safely on the Delaware River and was replaced by the Liston Range on October 24, 1904, after only twenty-seven years of service. The U.S. Lighthouse Service disassembled the rear light from the Port Penn Range and reestablished it as the rear light for the new Liston Range, but the Port Penn Range Front Light was not so fortunate.

Following the Port Penn Range Front Light going dark, the Lighthouse Service decided to sell the excess lighthouse and property at public auction on April 20, 1911. Lighthouse historian Jim Gowdy describes the next phase

Dedication of the Port Penn Range Front Light historic marker, June 14, 2003. *Left to right:* DRBLHF president Bob Trapani, Russ McCabe of Delaware Public Archives, Delaware Representative Richard Cathcart, Delaware State Representative Joseph DiPinto and Dr. William Duncan. *Photo by Ann-Marie Trapani.*

of the decommissioned light station's existence, saying, "After the former lighthouse was sold it soon became a rental property. The condition of the dwelling went downhill over time, and later the building was destroyed by fire. Exact details about the demise of the former lighthouse are not known." This would seem to have been the end of the Port Penn Range Front Light, as even the marshland that was reclaimed to support the historic lighthouse began "swallowing" the site with thick bushes, briars and phragmites.

As the years passed, even the very location of the former light station became obscured. If not for the efforts of one man, it is doubtful that today's lighthouse community would have ever been able to identify the fragmented remains of the lighthouse and oil house. Thanks to Dr. William H. Duncan of Wilmington, Delaware, not only has the location of the former light been found, but the sentinel's twenty-seven years of valuable service to mariners is now also officially recognized for posterity.

Finding the site of the former Port Penn Range Front Light was more than a random lighthouse quest for Dr. Duncan. In fact, strong family ties to the light station spurred Dr. Duncan's interest in retracing the sentinel's past and locating the time-forgotten site. The second keeper that was appointed at Port Penn Range Front Light was George Washington Duncan—Dr. William Duncan's grandfather—who served at the station from 1885 until 1904 when the range was decommissioned.

Following his discovery of the former lighthouse location, Dr. William Duncan led a two-year effort to obtain a historic marker to commemorate the importance of the former lighthouse site to the State of Delaware. A historic marker paying tribute to the site of the Port Penn Range Front Light was eventually unveiled and dedicated at the location on June 14, 2003. "With the completion of this project, an important chapter in Delaware's maritime history has been documented for all to see," said Russ McCabe of the Delaware State Archives. "The Port Penn project was a first of sorts—this being the first marker concerning lighthouse history that has been requested in the State of Delaware."

# Chapter 12

## Cherry Island Range Light Stations

### 1880

In an effort to satisfy the pleas of mariners on the Delaware River for navigation aids to guide vessels past the dangers of Cherry Island Flats near Edgemoor, the United States Lighthouse Service (USLHS) established the Cherry Island Range in 1880.

The first mention of Cherry Island Flats is found in the 1875 *Annual Report*, which reported to Congress, "There is a bad shoal at this point, with a narrow channel on either side. It should be marked by a light or lights, the exact positions of which can only be determined by a survey."

Another five years would pass before the Cherry Island Range was completed and first lit on April 1, 1880. Nearly a year later the USLHS would further improve the range's ability to safeguard ships passing the flats with the installation of a fog bell at the front light station on February 20, 1881. The bell, which sounded once every fifteen seconds, was located on the outer corner of the wharf, approximately one hundred feet from the shipping channel. An interesting historical note is that the fog bell was not new but relocated from the Delaware Breakwater West End Light when that station's bell was upgraded in size.

The 1881 *Annual Report* notes "a change in the lantern was made so as to allow an arc of illumination of 180 degrees." The report goes on to note that by changing the position of the illuminating apparatus, the "Christiana Light and this light form a range showing up the river, intersecting Schooner Ledge Range in deep water." It is unknown

# Cherry Island Range Light Stations, 1880

Cherry Island Range Front Light. *Courtesy of Jeremy D'Entremont.*

whether the optic was simply repositioned inside the lantern or the small lighthouse was moved along the wharf to create the additional benefit of the intersecting ranges.

A devastating fire destroyed the keeper's house at Cherry Island Range Front Light on August 8, 1891, though the U.S. Lighthouse Service provides no details of how the fire started. They did report to Congress that "measures were taken at once to rebuild the structure." The 1892 *Annual Report* confirms this action, noting that the dwelling destroyed by fire the previous year had been rebuilt.

The first mention of the light's characteristics being altered occurred on October 30, 1894, when the Cherry Island Range Front Light was changed from fixed white to fixed white during periods of two seconds, separated by eclipses of a one-second duration. The 1885 *Annual Report* notes that the tower's upper portion of the foundation was rebuilt, and the tower was relocated a few feet back from its former position to better form its navigational range. Two years later, a red sector was placed in the lantern, which was designed to show upstream and help prevent ships from straying too close the river's western bank.

The range front light station, which consisted of a keeper's dwelling, fog signal and detached light tower, grew in 1896–97 when a detached brick oil house was built. A unique improvement occurred during 1899–1900 when the U.S. Lighthouse Service decided to establish a separate stand in the lantern apart from the pedestal that supported the range lens. According to the 1900 *Annual Report*, "A pane of red glass was framed and mounted on the railing of the lantern balcony, and an auxiliary sixth-order lamp and lens were installed to illuminate the red sector."

In an effort to make the Cherry Island Range Front Light more outstanding amidst the outbuildings and buoys strewn along the Edgemoor Buoy Depot, the lighthouse service painted the keeper's dwelling, fog signal, oil house and the storehouses belonging to the buoy depot a light brown on June 17, 1901. The lighthouse remained white in color while the roofs of every building affected by the color scheme change remained reddish brown.

More changes to the optic at the front light occurred in 1901–02, when the red sector in the lantern was discontinued. The 1901 *Light List* notes that this light was equipped with a fifth-order lens showing a white light twenty-eight feet above high water. The tower was described as a two-story wooden structure painted white with lead-colored trimmings. The tower's roof and lantern were painted black. By 1905 the lighthouse had acquired a lean from settling, and though the problem was rectified, the U.S. Lighthouse Service began formulating plans for a new tower. On November 5, 1906, the lens occulting apparatus was removed from the stricken lighthouse and placed atop a temporary lantern.

Apparently the damage caused to the lighthouse by settling was not isolated but something that affected much of the wharf on which the beacon stood, necessitating the rebuilding of the wharf. The 1908 *Annual Report*, when commenting on the Edgemoor Lighthouse Depot status, noted, "The reconstruction of the south wharf will permit the moving of the house of the Cherry Island Range Front Light to the present position of the light. This light is at present in a small frame shed of unsightly appearance erected because the wharf was not strong enough to support the original house."

The historic lighthouse was rebuilt in 1912, but apparently its replacement was more in the style of an unmanned light tower, which was described as being a white, square, pyramidal, wooden tower. This same year, the light's optic was changed from the old oil-wick to acetylene, a change that generally spelled the end of a full-time keeper. In 1916 the acetylene system was replaced by electric incandescent.

The 1936 *Light List* notes that the unmanned light tower showed an occulting white light from a locomotive-type reflector every three seconds. The tower was listed as being thirty-five feet tall, with a focal plane of thirty-eight feet above the water. Today the Cherry Island Range Front Light remains in service, although the automated skeleton tower has been rebuilt on various occasions.

# Cherry Island Range Light Stations, 1880

Cherry Island Range Rear Light. *Lewes Historical Society.*

The Cherry Island Range Rear Light was a much more handsome and durable beacon than its counterpart. The range rear light went into service on April 1, 1880, and consisted of a 2½-story wooden dwelling, surmounted by a lantern. The 1881 *Annual Report* paints a rather "homey" picture at the rear light, stating, "The kitchen and sitting room walls were painted, and a number of shade trees were planted around the dwelling. The lantern, railing, and roof of lantern were painted black, and the metal roofs of the dwelling and porch were painted." The lighthouse, which was 45 feet tall from the ground to its lantern, exhibited a fixed white light from a height of 120 feet above water on the Delaware River.

Improvements to the light station continued in the ensuing years. The 1897 *Annual Report* notes that the lighthouse was thoroughly repaired and that a detached brick oil house was built to replace the wood-frame structure used for storing the light's fuel. Two years later, the Lighthouse Service erected a kitchen addition to the dwelling. The 1900 *Annual Report* cites the fact that "the addition to the lighthouse was completed. This is a frame structure, having a stone-wall foundation and a tin roof. The front veranda was remodeled and a rear veranda was built."

A December 20, 1907 inspection report of the light station by U.S. Lighthouse Service assistant engineer H. Bamber reveals some very good details about the Cherry Island Range Rear Light. According to the report the lighthouse was painted white with lead-colored trimmings, green shutters and a black lantern. The dwelling, which was surmounted by a lantern, contained seven rooms besides the hallways, pantry and watchroom. In addition to the lighthouse, the station consisted of a red brick oil house and privy and a frame barn. The size of the light station was estimated to be about two acres and contained ten fine maple, one walnut, one horse chestnut, eight cherry and seven apple trees, all of which were surrounded by a fence.

The report further noted that the beacon's light consisted of a twenty-two-inch parabolic reflector showing a fixed white light. In the absence of a pedestal, a wooden cupboard supported the lamp and reflector. The lamp itself was a headlight lamp with a single-wick fourth-order constant level burner. The oil for the lamp was kept in the eight-by-twelve-foot oil house, which was located about twenty-three feet north of the lighthouse.

The light source for the Cherry Island Range Rear Light was changed from an oil-wick to incandescent oil vapor during 1915–16, but the very next year an electric light replaced the incandescent oil vapor system. The lighthouse was automated around 1933, with the 1936 *Light List* noting the beacon was unmanned, showing a fixed white light from a range lens illuminated by electricity. The lighthouse itself was described as a white, square tower attached to the dwelling, with a white lantern and a black circular daymark affixed above the lantern.

The U.S. Coast Guard used the lighthouse to house an Aids to Navigation technician and his family until at least the mid-1960s. By 1970–71 the beacon for the Cherry Island Range Rear Light was moved to a modern skeleton tower and the old structure was decommissioned. The structure was no longer necessary for housing and a decision was made to raze the structure. Today the brick oil house remains the only vestige of the one-time historic light station. The U.S. Coast Guard Aids to Navigation Team Philadelphia continues to maintain both the modern front and rear towers of the Cherry Island Range.

# Chapter 13

# Delaware Breakwater Range Rear Light Station
## 1881

One of the most obscure lighthouses in Delaware history was built two miles north of Lewes amid an environmental paradise known as the Great Marsh. The Delaware Breakwater Range Rear Light, which towered 101½ feet above the ground, was a stark contrast to its surroundings of serene tidal waters, hummocks, marsh reeds and forests of pine, cedar and red maple.

The brown skeletal tower that composed the Delaware Breakwater Range Rear Light was constructed of wrought iron and first lit on November 1, 1881. The lighthouse worked in tandem with a front light to guide mariners through the channel around the sandy tip of Cape Henlopen and into the protective waters behind the Delaware Breakwater. For the first three years of the beacon's existence, it showed a fixed red beam, produced by a powerful third-order range lens. By October 1, 1884, the U.S. Lighthouse Service changed the color to a fixed white light in an effort to prevent it from being confused with the red sector in the nearby Cape Henlopen Light.

In addition to the tower at the site of the Delaware Breakwater Range Rear Light, the station also included a keeper's dwelling, brick oil house, frame barn, frame storehouse, frame privy and frame tank house. In an inspection report made by the Lighthouse Service on December 4, 1907, the lightkeeper's house was described as a wood-frame structure situated about fifteen feet off the southeast corner of the light tower. The house was

# Delaware Breakwater Range Rear Light Station, 1881

Delaware Breakwater Range Rear Light. *Robert Lewis collection.*

supported by a stone foundation and was painted white with lead-colored trimmings and green shutters. The oil house was the only outbuilding at the light station with a red roof.

A second dwelling was constructed in 1910 for the assistant keeper at the Delaware Breakwater Range Rear Light. The house itself was quite distinguished, as the single-story dwelling was constructed of concrete. In fact, the only other keeper's house in Delaware that was built of concrete was at the Bellevue Range Rear Light near Wilmington. Just two years later, the arrangement of maintaining two keepers at the light station was discontinued. At that time the original frame dwelling built in 1881 was deemed excess property and subsequently sold at auction between 1913 and 1915.

As early as October 1911, the U.S. Lighthouse Service was earnestly discussing a move to decommission the Delaware Breakwater Range Rear Light. The combination of the wealth of aids to navigation in and around the Delaware Breakwater Harbor and the ever extending sandy point of Cape Henlopen—which continued to migrate north-northwest—made this range unnecessary in the opinion of the federal government. The end finally came in 1918 when the light's guiding beam was permanently darkened, bringing a close to its short thirty-seven-year tenure.

Though the tower's service at Delaware Breakwater Range Rear Light was over, the lighthouse was to shine again at another light station. A letter

Concrete keeper's dwelling at Delaware Breakwater Range Rear Light. *Robert Lewis collection.*

dated January 25, 1919, from the Fourth Lighthouse District Superintendent W. Merritt to the commissioner of lighthouses, stated,

> *Two sets of range lights are needed for guiding vessels through the Boca Grande Entrance and into Charlotte Harbor. One set to indicate the axis of the dredged cut at the entrance and the other to mark the turning point and lead vessels into the harbor. Plans have been completed for a standard steel structure for Boca Grande Range Rear Light. This light is to be established on shore six miles from Charlotte Harbor Entrance Gas and Bell Buoy, and in the opinion of this office would be a very desirable location for this tower* [the former Delaware Breakwater Range Rear Light].

The uncertainty of where the Delaware Breakwater Range Rear Light eventually found a new home was due to a delay in the actual disassembling of the wrought-iron sentinel, which was caused by a lack of money in the Seventh Lighthouse District. Superintendent Merritt alluded to this in his January 25 letter to the commissioner of lighthouses, writing, "No funds are available in this district for dismantling the tower. However, the necessary funds could be deducted from the allotment to the Seventh District for the fiscal year 1920 when appropriated and available."

In the meantime, the darkened sentinel continued to stand silent watch over the Great Marsh until U.S. Lighthouse Service could budget the funds. A year would pass before the lighthouse was transitioned to its next assignment. The 1920 *Annual Report* notes that the Delaware Breakwater Range Rear Light was dismantled and placed on cars for rail shipment. Though the skeletal tower left Lewes bound for Florida, the tower remained in storage for the next seven years for whatever reason.

Since the lighthouse disappeared from the radar screen, the facts about the final destination of the Delaware Breakwater Range Rear Light became obscured as well. By 1927 the lighthouse reemerged on the Gulf Coast of Florida, where it became the Gasparilla Range Rear Light. The tower's color was changed from brown to white. Its lantern room showed a light from all sides, rather than in one direction like it had while serving as the Delaware Breakwater Range Rear Light. Many years would pass before lighthouse enthusiasts finally learned that the Delaware Breakwater Range Rear Light didn't simply just disappear, but that it lives on as a guiding light along Florida's Gulf Coast.

During the light's tenure in Delaware, it had the unique distinction of having worked in tandem with two separate range front lights located in different spots along the Delaware Breakwater—all without any of the three lighthouses being moved. The Delaware Breakwater West End Lighthouse served as the front light for the Delaware Breakwater Range from 1881 to 1903. However, a temporary light was established on the south end of the National Harbor of Refuge Breakwater, and the old West End Lighthouse was deemed obsolete and subsequently decommissioned. Following this change, the Delaware Breakwater East End Lighthouse, which was located on the easterly end of the inner breakwater, took over as the front light for the Delaware Breakwater Range. This arrangement lasted until 1918, when the advancement of the Cape Henlopen point rendered the range useless.

Today, remnants of the Delaware Breakwater Range Rear Light Station or Green Hill Light—as locals in Lewes refer to it—still exist but they are slowly being overtaken by the Great Marsh. The concrete keeper's dwelling, though its roof has collapsed and the interior of the structure deteriorated, the brick oil house and the concrete piers that form the giant footprint of the former skeletal tower that once presided over the site still exist. The Lewes Greenway and Trail Committee is working on a plan to interpret the former light station so that future generations will be able to learn about a bygone piece of Delaware's lighthouse heritage.

# Chapter 14

# Delaware Breakwater East End Light Station
# 1885

The story of the Delaware Breakwater East End Light Station cannot be told without first delving briefly into the history of the Delaware Breakwater's massive stone wall. At the time of its construction, the engineering marvel that yielded the eight-tenths-of-a-mile-long wall of protection off Cape Henlopen was the second largest such work of its kind in the world. Though the breakwater's value as a harbor of refuge proved immense for mariners caught in the midst of a northeast storm, the initial undertaking in the 1820s was more tied to the financial concerns and losses of Philadelphia and Delaware merchants than humanitarian aspects. Another political force lobbying Congress for a protective breakwater was the nation's War Department, which envisioned the stone wall as a huge benefit for its largest class of naval war vessels.

Congress appropriated $22,700 by the act of May 7, 1822, for "erecting in the bay of Delaware two piers of sufficient dimensions to be a harbor of shelter for vessels from the ice," but seven years would pass before the project began in earnest. Contractors finally dropped the first stones into the waters of the harbor in 1829, and forty years later, in 1869, the Delaware Breakwater was finally completed.

At the same time raging surf and shifting sands were steadily undermining the vulnerable Cape Henlopen Beacon Light on the nearby point of the cape; plans were being made by the U.S. Lighthouse Service in 1884 to transfer the duties of the doomed lighthouse and fog-signal station out

# Delaware Breakwater East End Light Station, 1885

Delaware Breakwater East End Lighthouse. *National Archives.*

onto the Delaware Breakwater. By April 5, 1885, the Delaware Breakwater East End Light Station construction process progressed to the point that a temporary light fifty feet above mean low water could be exhibited from the site. The 1885 *Annual Report* stated, "The lantern is of the fourth order, and is fitted with a red panel to correspond in all aspects with the permanent beacon which is to replace it."

On October 2, 1885, the temporary beacon was discontinued and the newly constructed Delaware Breakwater East End Lighthouse illuminated for the first time. By November of the same year, a Daboll trumpet fog signal was established at the light station, thus replacing the steam fog signal station at the former Cape Henlopen Beacon Light. The Delaware Breakwater East End Lighthouse was a brown conical cast-iron tower that stands fifty-six feet tall from its base to the cupola. According to the 1945 *Light List*, the actual light source was displayed sixty-one feet above the water, factoring in the height of the breakwater wall on which it is built. The Delaware Breakwater East End Lighthouse was fitted with a fourth-order Fresnel lens and showed a fixed white light seaward for approximately thirteen miles. Red panels or sectors were placed in the lantern room to warn mariners of a dangerous shoal just off Cape Henlopen as ships entered the Breakwater Harbor.

The Delaware Breakwater East End Lighthouse was established or "rooted" into the stone breakwater at a depth of eleven feet after contractors excavated the stone from the site and poured a concrete foundation to support the structure. The interior of the lighthouse contained six levels within a tapered cylinder lined with brick. Lightkeepers entered the structure from the west side of the breakwater and walked into a work area for machinery. This entry level housed two generators for the optic and two compressors for the foghorn. The duplicate arrangement enabled the keepers to stagger the workload on each unit and have a backup on hand for those times when a piece of machinery malfunctioned.

The second level housed the kitchen and office area and the third and fourth levels were sleeping quarters for the keepers and the occasional laborer. The first four levels of the lighthouse had a diameter of approximately eighteen feet, so the living area within the structure became quite confining for the lightkeepers—especially during the long, bitter cold days of winter when the keepers were restricted to indoor activities.

The fifth level of the lighthouse served as the watchroom. Before the advent of electricity, lightkeepers would maintain an all-night vigil in this room to ensure the incandescent oil-vapor light stayed lit for mariners seeking the guiding beams of the light. The room was sparsely furnished and contained built-in cabinets that housed spare equipment and materials for the lens and a small desk and chair where the keeper would maintain his watch and logbook. This level also possessed an exterior gallery for lightkeepers to walk outside and assess their surroundings. The last level was the lantern room where the classical prism lens was located.

Though the value of the lighthouse was highly appreciated for its visual help to vessels entering Delaware Breakwater Harbor, ship captains considered the sentinel's "voice" paramount during times of thick weather or dense fog. No light station in Delaware Bay history made more noise in an effort to warn mariners of sightless waterborne dangers than Delaware Breakwater East End. In the first full two years of operation—1886 and 1887—the fog signal sounded its ear-piercing warning 898 and 912 hours, respectively. During these hours of operation, the lightkeeper was feeding the Daboll trumpet fog signal an average of six tons of coal per year.

The Delaware Breakwater East End Lighthouse performed a variety of functions as an aid to navigation in an effort to warn mariners of the dangers approaching Cape Henlopen and inside the Delaware Breakwater Harbor. In 1903 the lighthouse took over the duties of the Delaware Breakwater West End Lighthouse when the latter was decommissioned. This arrangement remained in place until 1918, when the range was

# Delaware Breakwater East End Light Station, 1885

Delaware Breakwater East End Lighthouse. *Lewes Historical Society.*

deemed unnecessary. At this point, the Delaware Breakwater East End Light went back to serving as a lighthouse marking the inner harbor.

As the years passed and the breakwater grew less important for protecting shipping, the option of automating the Delaware Breakwater East End Light became attractive to the Coast Guard. A letter dated June 12, 1950, from the desk of the commander of the Third Coast Guard District, stated, "The added burden of transportation of aids to navigation personnel and the maintenance of aids to navigation quite frequently leaves the Lewes Lifeboat Station short of personnel should an emergency occur. In view of the above, it is recommended that two of the personnel now authorized for Delaware Light Station be assigned to Lewes Lifeboat Station in order that the station may perform its search and rescue duties in a more efficient manner."

This recommendation was carried through, and the last resident Coast Guard lightkeepers were ordered to leave the Delaware Breakwater East End Lighthouse. A Coast Guard memo dated July 20, 1950, was very brief in conveying this change at the lighthouse, as it simply stated, "The light station was changed to unwatched on 11 July 1950."

Another interesting chapter in the history of the Delaware Breakwater East End Lighthouse was the occupation of the structure by the Pilots' Association for the Bay and River Delaware. The Pilots' Association is an organization of professional captains who guide large commercial vessels safely up and down the Delaware River and Bay to the tri-state ports of call. Prior to 1979, the Pilots did not have a land-based operation at the Delaware Capes to operate during emergencies or when the Pilot boat *Philadelphia* would need to go into dry dock for routine maintenance. Their entire operation at the mouth of the Delaware Bay was controlled from the water aboard their vessels.

A letter dated October 8, 1962, from the Pilots' President W.R. Egan to the commander of the Third Coast Guard District conveyed their intentions to occupy the Delaware Breakwater East End Lighthouse as a base of operations during times of necessity. The letter stated,

> *Dear Admiral, we are interested in the possibility of our Association being able to use the facilities of the old breakwater lighthouse at Delaware Breakwater. The light is unmanned and the quarters are not being used. We wanted the facility as an emergency point of operation if it would become necessary. We would use it at least during times when our big boat is in the shipyard or has to leave the station. I would be glad to come to New York and talk this over with you and explain more in detail our reasons for this request and get your views on the matter, if you so wish.*

The Coast Guard eventually approved of this arrangement in February 1963, with the stipulation that their servicing personnel have access to the lighthouse for maintaining the light source, electrical panels, timers, fog signal and emergency generators. The Coast Guard retained the responsibility of all costs associated with keeping the light in the lantern room working properly and for maintaining the exterior of the structure. The Pilots' Association would utilize the Delaware Breakwater East End Lighthouse as a substitute base of operations well into the 1970s.

By the mid-1990s, the Delaware Breakwater East End Lighthouse was deemed unnecessary as an aid to navigation by the Coast Guard and was decommissioned in September 1996. The General Services Administration eventually deeded ownership of the lighthouse from the federal government to the State of Delaware on February 5, 1999. The Delaware Division of Historical & Cultural Affairs leased the lighthouse to the Delaware River & Bay Authority (DRBA) on November 12, 2001. The lease agreement presented an opportunity to ensure the light's preservation and enable the historic site to be used as an educational resource for the general public.

# Delaware Breakwater East End Light Station, 1885

On September 30, 2004, the Delaware River & Bay Authority publicly announced a working partnership with the nonprofit Delaware River & Bay Lighthouse Foundation. DRBA Executive Director James T. Johnson noted, "In August [2004] our organization authorized an operating agreement with the DRBLHF to preserve and maintain the Delaware Breakwater East End Lighthouse, and to establish an educational outreach program. The Authority, the State of Delaware and the Lighthouse Foundation recognize the historical importance and cultural value this lighthouse played in the local maritime community."

# Chapter 15

# Fourteen Foot Bank Light Station
## 1887

Fourteen Foot Bank Light Station holds the distinction of being the first lighthouse in the United States to be built on a submarine foundation using the pneumatic process in 1886–87. The lighthouse is also the only caisson sentinel situated along the main shipping channel of the Delaware Bay that resides in Delaware waters. Located on the western side of the sea lane a few miles offshore of Bower's Beach in Delaware, the beacon was deemed necessary by maritime interests to mark not only Fourteen Foot Bank Shoal over which it stood, but also Brown Shoal to the south and Joe Flogger Shoal to the north.

Before this caisson lighthouse was built, the first lighted aid to be established at Fourteen Foot Bank Shoal was lightship no. 19, which was placed on station to mark the dangerous shoal on August 22, 1876. The lightship usually had no problem maintaining its position throughout spring, summer and fall, but the winter was an entirely different story. Nearly every year the lightship was in service from 1876 to 1886, running ice floes either carried the vessel off station or forced it to seek protection at Delaware Breakwater, some twenty miles southward at the mouth of the bay.

The 1878 *Annual Report* noted, "With heavy ice running in the bay it is impossible to keep her in place, and in importance it is second to none in the bay and river. A lighthouse should be built on the lower end of Joe Flogger Shoal. This would enable the board to withdraw the lightship. The estimated cost of the lighthouse is $150,000, but the cost of maintenance is much less than that of a lightship."

Another eight years would pass before the lightship was finally removed from Fourteen Foot Bank Shoal on December 1, 1886. During

Fourteen Foot Bank Lighthouse sporting its brown daymark. *National Archives.*

this time the caisson lighthouse was completed sufficiently to display a temporary light at the site. Workmen built a makeshift platform that spanned the caisson cylinder and established a fixed white fourth-order lantern and apparatus as a temporary beacon. Coincidentally, this very same fourth-order lantern had previously served as the temporary light for the Delaware Breakwater East End Lighthouse just a year earlier in 1885. In addition to the lantern, a ship's fog bell was also installed. Since the superstructure for the lighthouse had yet to be completed, workmen built a temporary frame dwelling on the concrete floor inside the caisson cylinder to house the station's lightkeepers.

The engineering challenges associated with the establishment of what the United States Lighthouse Service (USLHS) described as an "immense pier" or caisson cylinder are worth a closer look. The foundation was built by a contractor and stored in Lewes, Delaware, before the site was prepared to receive it. The cylinder was built in 12 courses, each containing 36 iron plates measuring 1½ inches in thickness. The sheer size of the cylinder was amazing, as it stood 73 feet tall and 35 feet in diameter, including 30 feet visible above the waterline.

According to the 1884 *Annual Report*, "The intention was to have sunk the foundation in place during the coming summer [1884], and preparations were made therefor, but so many difficulties were encountered in the experimental stages of the work that it was deemed best to defer its erection till the summer of 1885." Once the USLHS completed its survey of the site in July 1884, engineers determined that the caisson could only be properly established on the shoal through the pneumatic process.

On July 5, 1885, the wooden caisson foundation with three tiers of the iron cylinder erected upon it was towed from Lewes to the shoal and submerged into position by allowing water into it. Once the cylinder was sunk, workers used compressed air to penetrate the shoal and "root" the foundation firmly in place. In all, the caisson was sunk to the required depth of twenty-three feet, and when the cast-iron plates forming the cylinder were complete, two thousand cubic yards of concrete were used to fill the interior. The eventual total cost to build Fourteen Foot Bank Light Station was $123,811.45.

The winter season was not kind to the site as a variety of factors resulted in the increase of water depth atop the shoal. The 1886 *Annual Report* noted, "To prevent the sand from scouring out from around the base of the cylinder, 1,000 tons of riprap were put in place during November. The water is now 24 feet deep here at low tide, while it was but 20 feet deep when the work was begun at the site. During the winter the pier was frequently struck by large fields of floating ice, and at times the vibrations knocked articles from the table and cooking utensils from the stove."

Winter's ice floe would continue to assault the lighthouse throughout the beacon's history. More than one former keeper cited the unnerving experience of coping with powerful fields of ice slamming against the lighthouse and causing the structure to shudder ceaselessly. Often the keeper's furniture would literally vibrate across the floor due to the shock of the frozen cakes hitting the lighthouse. One keeper reported that during a particularly severe run of ice floes, he awoke the next morning to find his bed moved completely to the other side of the room from the structure constantly shuddering.

Though the winter of 1886–87 was a tough one, contractors persevered and eventually completed the light's superstructure on January 22, 1887, with the exception of dwellings, exterior paint and other minor details. In mid-April 1887, the temporary light was removed and the beacon's permanent light—a fourth-order Fresnel lens exhibiting a flashing white light every fifteen seconds with red sectors to mark Brown and Joe Flogger Shoals—was lit for the first time. The lighthouse later received a second-class Daboll trumpet fog signal in September 1887, at which time the project of painting the superstructure was completed.

Five years later, the 1892 *Annual Report* noted that the Fourteen Foot Bank's flashing light was changed to a fixed beam, which was described by the USLHS as "Fixed for a period of forty seconds' duration, followed successively, by an eclipse of three seconds, fixed period of fourteen seconds, and eclipse of three seconds, fixed period of fourteen seconds, and an eclipse of three seconds. Neither the order of the light nor the red sector was changed."

Over the years it was as if Fourteen Foot Bank Lighthouse was the chameleon of Delaware Bay sentinels. Originally, the lighthouse's exterior color scheme, or its daymark, was painted entirely chocolate brown, which lasted until about 1908. At some point later through 1931 the entire cylinder and superstructure were painted black in color. Mariners probably could not help viewing Fourteen Foot Bank Light from the bridge of ship at this time—especially during the icy winter months—and not feel a gripping sense of desolation and depression conjured up by the station's remote location and eerie black daymark. The U.S. Coast Guard would eventually change the light's color scheme in 1941 to a white superstructure trimmed in black, with its caisson cylinder painted black.

The 1908 *Light List* notes that Fourteen Foot Bank Lighthouse showed fifty-nine feet above the water, while its Daboll trumpet fog

Fourteen Foot Bank Lighthouse. *Photo by Bob Trapani Jr.*

signal sounded a blast for four seconds before falling silent for four more seconds. The publication goes on to describe the lighthouse as a "cylindrical foundation expanding in trumpet shape under [the] main gallery, surmounted by a two-story dwelling with gable roof; tower, surmounted by lantern, rises from [the] easterly side of dwelling." The entire superstructure, which is in the Classic Revival style, is constructed of cast iron.

In 1912 the light's illuminating apparatus was changed from the old-style oil wick to a more efficient incandescent oil vapor system, followed by a new revolving lens in 1918. By 1936 the U.S. Lighthouse Service *Light List* noted that Fourteen Foot Bank Lighthouse showed a group-occulting, flashing white light (two flashes every ten seconds) with a red sector. The light's candlepower was 20,000 white and 6,000 red, with the white light visible up to thirteen nautical miles. The station's fog signal consisted of a diaphone air horn that sounded one blast for five seconds before falling silent for twenty-five seconds. Interestingly, the light's superstructure was described as being painted white, and its cylindrical foundation painted the color red.

The great northeaster of March 6–8, 1962, was one of the most powerful Delaware storms on record. Though rain fell during the storm and strong winds blew approximately fifty-five miles per hour, with gusts up to seventy-two miles per hour, it was the wind-driven seas and five successive high tides up to nine feet above normal that made this unnamed storm so destructive. So what was it like to be on a Delaware Bay lighthouse during the northeast tempest? According to Lewes resident Warren Walls, who was the officer-in-charge at Fourteen Foot Bank at the time, not very much fun. In fact the whole experience was disturbing enough to make a lasting impression.

"There wasn't any indication of a storm coming prior to its arrival," said Walls. "It was very foggy for a week before the storm hit. I remember the fog horn blew 18 to 22 hours a day during that time." The first indications of a storm's approach—though no one could know just how severe this northeaster would turn out to be—were revealed the night of March 5. By the morning of the sixth, the lightkeepers would find themselves thrown into a world of frightening chaos with no place to hide.

Warren Walls went on to say, "The waves were so high that they were washing up over the caisson cylinder onto the main deck and flooding the basement of the lighthouse. We had to close the main door covers; however, they were rusty and frozen open because we never used them. This ended up being a task unto itself because of the seas washing up on the main deck. During the storm the lighthouse shook and vibrated terribly. I thought I would never get off the light alive and knew all too well that no one or any boat or plane could get us off." Fourteen Foot Bank Light held its ground in the face of the harrowing tempest, but the experience was something Walls and his fellow crewmembers will never forget.

Fourteen Foot Bank Lighthouse was finally automated in 1973 and is presently maintained by the United States Coast Guard as an active aid to navigation. The lighthouse contains a modern 300mm acrylic optic and FA/232 fog signal to help guide mariners, each powered by solar energy. The light's classical fourth-order Fresnel lens was removed in the late 1990s and placed on loan to the Lewes Historical Society, which houses the beautiful artifact in the Cannonball House.

Today Fourteen Foot Bank Lighthouse not only serves mariners on Delaware Bay but also the general public as a marine research platform for the University of Delaware's College of Marine Studies. The lighthouse has served as a base of operations for the university's Delaware Bay Observing System since the late 1990s, which includes onsite meteorological instruments and water column measuring systems that continuously collect weather and oceanographic data. This invaluable data is then relayed electronically from the lighthouse to the College of Marine Studies campus in Lewes.

Other than the navigational equipment aboard Fourteen Foot Bank Lighthouse, the historic structure itself was deemed excess property by the U.S. Coast Guard in 2005 and placed into the National Historic Lighthouse Preservation Act (NHLPA) application process. The NHLPA is a federal program facilitated by the National Park Service and the General Services Administration that enables interested governmental agencies and nonprofits to be on equal footing in competing for the ownership of historic lighthouses.

In December 2005, the nonprofit American Lighthouse Foundation (ALF), a national lighthouse preservation organization headquartered in Wells, Maine, submitted an NHLPA application to the National Park Service in an effort to obtain ownership of Fourteen Foot Bank Lighthouse. As part of their application, ALF informed the National Park Service of their intent to partner with the College of Marine Studies to ensure that their university's marine science research program would continue, while demonstrating an alternative use for an offshore lighthouse like Fourteen Foot Bank. The federal government's decision on the light's future is expected by the end of 2006.

# Chapter 16

# Baker Range Light Stations 1904

aker Range is one of those cases in Delaware lighthouse history where a light station was established to mark an altered waterway. In 1901 the Army Corps of Engineers dredged a 20,500-foot section of the Delaware River opposite Appoquinimink Creek, to a depth of 30 feet. During the improvement process, the path of the previous channel was altered, necessitating the U.S. Lighthouse Service to make adjustments to range lights along the affected section of the waterway. Subsequently, the Port Penn Range, south of Augustine Beach, was decommissioned when the new Baker Range was established approximately two miles to the north.

The Baker Range has the distinction of being one of the shortest ranges in total length on the Delaware River. At only 1.65 miles long, river pilots no sooner steer on this range with large commercial ships before finding it necessary to turn toward the next range as they transit to the ports of call northward. Retired Delaware River pilot Captain Paul Ives describes the purpose of the range, saying, "Baker Range is a principal leg of the main channel which has to be transited before reaching Reedy Island Range, at the top of which is the entrance to the C&D Canal and Delaware City."

The temporary lights forming the new Baker Range were originally established and lit for the first time on November 11, 1902. A permanent two-story lighthouse was eventually constructed at the site of the front light for the Baker Range and lit on September 16, 1904. The location of this lighthouse was hardly ideal, as not only was the station isolated and accessible only by a levee, the mud flats were also prone to flooding and invasion by pesky mosquitoes and biting flies during the warmer months. The low-

Baker Range Front Light. *Courtesy of Harry Spencer Jr.*

lying area required the station to have elevated boardwalks connecting the lighthouse to other outbuildings such as the privy, oil house and barn.

A 1907 U.S. Lighthouse Service inspection report notes that the lighthouse was "located just inside the levee, on the westerly bank of the Delaware River, about ⅔ mile above Reedy Island…the site of the lighthouse is on a low meadow just inside of the river levee. The surface of the ground is only about 1½ feet above that of mean low water outside of the levee."

The Baker Range Front Light did not possess the traditional appearance of a lighthouse, rather consisted of a wood frame dwelling painted white, with a brown roof and lead-colored trimmings. The lighthouse rested on iron piles and showed a light to mariners from a second-story window nineteen feet above the water. The lighthouse had no watchroom since a portion of the second floor was partitioned off to form a lantern inside the house.

When originally established, Baker Range Front Light was equipped with a curtain occulting apparatus that revealed a fixed white light for two seconds before eclipsing it for one second. The optic consisted of a reflector lens with a locomotive-type headlight lamp illuminated by an oil wick.

# Baker Range Light Stations, 1904

Baker Range Rear Light. *Photo by Bob Trapani Jr.*

The original lighthouse served until 1924, when automation came to the Baker Range. A steel skeleton tower was established as the front light for the range on the southern tip of Reedy Island in the middle of the Delaware River. The demise of the Baker Range Front Light remains a mystery; at some point after 1929, it disappeared. It is unknown whether it was sold at auction, its construction materials salvaged or if it was burned by vandals. Only the iron pilings that once supported the lighthouse remain, nearly obscured today by the wild marsh.

Only one keeper was assigned to Baker Range, which must have made tending this range very undesirable. Regardless of the oppressive summer heat or icy cold of winter, the keeper was required to not only tend the beacon at the range's front light, but also the rear light. The lightkeeper had to walk a distance of 1.5 miles northward along a levee at least twice a day to extinguish the rear light at sunrise, and illuminate it again at dusk. This meant that the keeper walked a minimum of six miles each day—and often times more—no matter what the weather conditions. To make matters worse, the keeper also had to carry heavy cans of oil since there was no oil house to store it at the site of the rear light.

The permanent tower for the Baker Range Rear Light was established and first lit on April 23, 1906. The 110-foot triangular skeleton tower—shaped like a pyramid—has the distinction of serving as the rear light at the old Reedy Island Range in Port Penn from 1896 to 1904 before it was discontinued and replaced by the Baker Range. The Lighthouse Service simply disassembled the iron sentinel and moved it two miles north to its new location in the spring of 1905.

The tower, standing a lonely post within the broad expanse of the Thousand Acre Marsh, was painted brown and rested on six cement piers. It was located only about 70 feet inside a levee west of the waters on the Delaware. According to the USLHS 1907 inspection report, the skeleton beacon was equipped with a "small wooden lamp house and hoisting apparatus" that the keepers would raise up each night to display the tower's guiding light. The original optic consisted of a 22-inch reflector with a locomotive-type headlight lamp and an oil wick. The focal plane was 56½ feet and later raised to 89 feet.

The Baker Range remains active on the Delaware River and is maintained by the United States Coast Guard Aids to Navigation Team in Philadelphia, Pennsylvania. The historic 1896 skeleton tower continues to serve at the site of the range rear light and shows a fixed green light for modern ships transiting the Delaware River.

# Chapter 17

# Reedy Island Range Light Stations
## 1904

The Reedy Island Range was established in 1904 to mark the Delaware River's main shipping channel between Baker Shoal and Reedy Island. The U.S. Lighthouse Service (USLHS) originally intended for this range to replace the Finns Point Range on the New Jersey side of the Delaware River, following changes made to the shipping channel in 1901. In fact, the rear light of the Finns Point Range was to be disassembled and re-erected as part of the Reedy Island Range, but a decision was later made by the USLHS to maintain the New Jersey range in addition to establishing the new range along the west riverbank of the Delaware.

The Reedy Island Range Front Light, which stood approximately one hundred feet from water's edge, was situated on marshy ground between the Appoquinimink River to the west and Blackbird Creek to the southeast. Few other lighthouses along the Delaware River were considered more desolate, for there were no roads that led to this light station; there was only a thirty-two-foot-long footbridge that crossed what the U.S. Lighthouse Service referred to in their 1906 *Annual Report* as "Light-House Creek." In light of the station's remote location, few people ever saw this lighthouse outside of the families of keepers, mariners and fishermen.

The first light to shine from Reedy Island Range Front Light was a fixed white temporary light that was exhibited on February 16, 1904. The optic was a locomotive-type headlight resting atop a wooden lantern post that showed a light twenty feet above the water. Construction began

Reedy Island Range Front Light. *National Archives.*

during October 1905 on the permanent lighthouse and its outbuildings, which would consist of an oil house, boathouse and privy connected by an elevated walkway.

The twenty-nine-foot-tall lighthouse—which was a square two-story wood-frame dwelling painted white with lead-colored trimmings, green blinds, brown roof and a porch that wrapped completely around the house—was lit for the first time a year later on October 25, 1906. The reflector light from the nearby temporary post was removed and installed inside the lighthouse. The lantern and keeper's dwelling were integrated, with the lantern being located on the front slope of the roof showing a fixed white light from a focal plane of thirty-one feet.

Despite the light station's lonely location the United States Lighthouse Service recognized two of its keepers for their dedication to duty and humanitarian service between the years 1915 and 1921. Lightkeeper Arthur W. Hopkins was awarded the service's prestigious "Efficiency Flag" for the best-kept station for the calendar year 1915. Three years later keeper John E. Collins was awarded the same honor in 1918 for his dedication and hard work at Reedy Island Range Front Light.

In addition, keeper Collins was recognized three separate times in the service's *Annual Report* to Congress during the fiscal years of 1920 and 1921 for rendering assistance to recreational boaters who broke down or ran aground near the station. In each incident, the keeper went out of his way to either fix the mechanical problem or tow the boats to safety.

The 1936 *Light List* notes that the front beacon, which contained a range lens illuminated by incandescent oil vapor, showed an occulting white light every three seconds—lit for two seconds, eclipsed for one second. The 1945 *Light List* reports the beacon showing a flashing white light every three seconds and illuminated by acetylene. In addition, the Reedy Island Range was listed as being lit twenty-four hours a day. The 1945 *Light List* did not designate the light station as being "unwatched," so the mystery of when the station was automated and its keeper removed remains unsolved.

Automation certainly had come to Reedy Island Range Front Light in 1951 when the U.S. Coast Guard darkened the beacon inside the historic lighthouse and established a skeletal tower closer to water's edge to serve as the range's new front light. The Coast Guard then subdivided the property in 1952, with most of the land later becoming a parcel within the present-day Appoquinimink Wildlife Area. The final demise of the Reedy Island Range Front Light also remains a mystery. According to lighthouse historian James Gowdy, the prevailing thought is that the Coast Guard burned the lighthouse and its outbuildings to the ground at some point in the 1950s. Today only the cast-iron columns that once supported the lighthouse remain as a reminder to the light station's existence.

The Reedy Island Range Rear Light is located 2½ miles behind the front light in an area known as Taylor's Bridge. The historic 125-foot black skeletal tower looks out of place along Delaware's Route 9, towering above the surrounding farm fields and houses—so much so that people often do not know what to make of the structure, which isn't thought to be a lighthouse at all because of its nontraditional appearance and distance from the water.

The first light shown from this site was a locomotive-type reflector shown from a temporary 102-foot-tall wooden pole on February 16, 1904. The pole was also outfitted with a triangular slatted daymark painted black to help ship captains line up the range during daylight hours. The temporary light would remain in service for six years until the permanent lighthouse was completed and first lit on July 27, 1910.

In the late 1800s, the U.S. Lighthouse Service utilized wrought iron to construct skeleton lights like the rear lights at Liston Range and Finns

Reedy Island Range Rear Light. *Photo by Herb Von Goerres.*

Point Range, but for both economical and technological reasons, Reedy Island Range Rear Light was constructed primarily of cast iron. The tower rests on nine concrete piers and contains a central tube housing a narrow staircase that extends from its base to the watchroom. According to the National Register of Historic Places nomination form, "The pipe sections which make up both the vertical and horizontal members of the tower are held together by diagonal tie-rods running between cast-iron junctions. Horizontal members are in two parts jointed in the middle through large circular flanges."

The original optic for the lighthouse was a fifth-order range lens, illuminated by a fourth-order incandescent oil vapor lamp. The light shone through the northeast face of the tower from a focal plane of 134 feet above the water. Though the range faced ships transiting downriver toward the Delaware Bay, vessels transiting upriver to the tri-state ports of Delaware, Pennsylvania and New Jersey could utilize the range by viewing it from astern.

In addition to the tower, the light station consisted of a keeper's dwelling, a small barn, a glazed brick oil shed and a farm shed. The National Register nomination form described the wood-frame keeper's dwelling as a "two-story hip-roofed clapboard house of cruciform plan." The form went on to state that the house contained a front porch with Tuscan columns and a rail of turned balusters.

Tending a light at a station like the inland Reedy Island Range Rear Light was not an easy task, despite being protected from the scourge of storm surge. No one knew this better than keeper Aaron Kimmey, who served from 1911 to 1927, the longest tenure at the light station. During the height of summer, lightkeeper Kimmey was forced to climb the narrow staircase contained within the cast-iron central column tube of the skeleton tower several times a day to perform normal maintenance and prepare the light for evening illumination. With few windows for ventilation and the fact that the cast-iron held the heat, the air inside the tower became suffocating as temperatures could rise as high as 120 degrees.

The days of full-time keepers tending the light at Reedy Island Range Rear Light were numbered as the mid-1930s approached. Because of its more convenient inland location, the lighthouse was an easy station to electrify. Though the 1934 *Light List* states the rear light was equipped with a range lens illuminated by incandescent oil vapor and thus requiring a keeper to tend the light, the 1936 *Light List* notes that the station was illuminated by electricity.

Looking down from the lighthouse at the charred remains of the keeper's house and oil house that were destroyed by fire on April 6, 2002. *Photo by Bob Trapani Jr.*

The *Light List* publications do not mention the year, but sometime in the late 1930s the lighthouse was fully automated. According to Harry E. Spencer Jr. of Lewes, Delaware, his father—Harry E. Spencer Sr., keeper of the nearby Liston Range Front Light in Bayview Beach—was given responsibility for checking on Reedy Island Range Rear Light. "I remember my dad would make monthly visits to the range rear lights at Reedy Island and Liston in the late 1930s once both towers were automated," said the younger Spencer. "He would care for the light source, perform other minor housecleaning tasks and always install two new fresh lamps in the lampchanger, regardless if they were burned out or not."

Following automation, the federal government eventually divested itself of the keeper's dwelling, oil house and farm shed, which were sold into private ownership. Over the years the condition of the former keeper's house deteriorated as it sat abandoned for a time. A mysterious fire of unknown origins finally destroyed the former keeper's dwelling and severely damaged the nearby glazed brick oil house on April 6, 2002. The nonprofit Delaware Wild Lands acquired the former light station property, except the small parcel of land on which the lighthouse stood in the aftermath of the fire that destroyed much of the station's historic fabric.

The lighthouse itself was finally listed in the National Register of Historic Places on March 27, 1989. Reedy Island Range is maintained by the U.S. Coast Guard Aids to Navigation Team Philadelphia and continues to serve mariners on the Delaware River.

# Chapter 18

# Liston Range Light Stations
# 1906

The 1904 changes brought about by dredging a deeper channel in the Delaware River from Appoquinimink Creek to Reedy Point forced the decommissioning of the Port Penn Range and created the need for the establishment of the new Liston Range nearby on October 25, 1904. The front light for the Liston Range resides in Bayview Beach on the riverbanks of the Delaware, while the rear light stands three miles inland—seemingly out of place amid sprawling cornfields and nearby residential developments. Together, the two lights have the distinction of forming the longest navigable range in the United States, and possibly the world. Liston Range's white lights can be seen by ships twenty miles away as they help navigate the safe waters of the Delaware River's midchannel.

The first beacon to show from the Liston Range Front Light Station was a modest short-term light pole until the lighthouse structure could be completed. The 1905 *Annual Report* describes the first light, stating, "a temporary lantern carrying a triangular slatted daymark and a galvanized iron headlight was erected on October 25, 1904, when the light was exhibited for the first time." The first keeper of the Liston Range Front Light was none other than George Washington Duncan, who was the well-respected keeper of the decommissioned Port Penn Range, which the Liston Range took the place of in 1904. Keeper Duncan continued to live at the discontinued Port Penn Range Front Light while tending the temporary lantern at Liston Range Front Light until 1906.

The 1909 *Annual Report* comments on the completion of the light station, saying, "This light, located 4⅝ miles northwesterly from Liston's Point, was moved 78 feet northwesterly along its range line, and established in the

# Liston Range Light Stations, 1906

Liston Range Front Light under construction in 1907-08. *Courtesy of Dr. William Duncan.*

white two-story frame structure, surmounted by a watchroom and lantern, completed in November 1908. The illuminating apparatus is a locomotive headlight reflector, showing an occulting light. The permanent light, which had a focal plane of 50-feet above the water, was shown from the new structure for the first time on December 28, 1908."

Once completed, the Liston Range Front Light was described as white with lead-colored trimmings, green blinds and a metallic brown roof, located approximately 140 feet from the reaches of the Delaware River. The lighthouse was constructed of wood except for its tin roof. A frame barn and glazed brick oil house rounded out the government-built buildings at the light station.

Though records are inconclusive, it appears that the headlight reflector light that was originally installed inside the lantern room of the lighthouse in 1908 may have been in service for about eight years before a Fresnel range lens was supplied to the beacon. The first mention of a lens change at Liston Range Front Light was in 1916 when the *Report of the Commissioner of Lighthouses* briefly stated, "New lens installed."

No lighthouse keeper had more of a hand in writing the history of Liston Range than Harry E. Spencer Sr., who tended lights on the Delaware River and Bay and on the coast of New Jersey for a total of thirty-eight years.

Lightkeeper Spencer served fourteen years at Liston Range Rear Light from 1913 to 1927 and another sixteen years at Liston Range Front Light from 1927 to 1943. During this thirty-year period, the Spencer name was synonymous with Liston Range. In fact, keeper Spencer's commitment for maintaining one of the best light stations in the Fourth District earned him the coveted U.S. Lighthouse Service silver star efficiency pin for twelve straight quarters in the late 1930s.

Harry Spencer Jr. spoke about his father's incredible dedication as a lightkeeper: "My father would not settle for anything but the best the light station could be—everything had to be just right. He devoted his life to the duties of being an excellent lighthousekeeper, as well as to being a wonderful husband and father to his family."

Keeper Spencer might have been the official person in charge of Liston Range Front Light, but by no means was he a one-man show. His wife Sophia played a huge role in keeper Spencer's recognition from the Lighthouse Service for having the best-kept light station. "Dad didn't win his awards by himself—mom was a big part of it too," said Spencer Jr. When the inspector would appear at the lighthouse to examine the station, he wouldn't simply look at the light source, lens and exterior of the structure. He also would carefully inspect every facet of the interior of the lighthouse for any trace of dust and overall cleanliness and order.

When keeper Spencer unexpectedly passed away in June 1943, Liston Range Front Light received its final lightkeeper—Sophia Spencer. The United States Coast Guard, which assumed America's lighthouses from the U.S. Lighthouse Service in 1939, thought so much of keeper Spencer's service that they decided to appoint his wife Sophia as a lamplighter for the next five years from 1943 until her retirement in 1948.

Following Sophia Spencer's retirement in 1948, the Coast Guard automated the historic lighthouse and by 1953 the lighthouse itself became victim to more cost-efficient methods. Rather than try to maintain the historic structure for a simple light, the Coast Guard decided to erect a modern steel skeleton tower in front of the lighthouse in 1953 to serve as the front light of Liston Range. Once the light was removed from the lighthouse, the Coast Guard quickly sold the historic structure. Mrs. Kathleen Herbert became the first private owner of Liston Range Front Light when she purchased the site at auction in 1954 for $8,200. Eleanor and Ernest Hardin eventually become the owners of the lighthouse until they too sold the site in 1998.

When Dr. William and Doris Duncan purchased Liston Range Front Light in January 1998, the light station's history came full circle. Dr. Duncan is the grandson of George Washington Duncan, the very first lightkeeper

Keeper Harry Spencer Sr. and his son Harry Jr. in 1938. *Courtesy of Harry Spencer Jr.*

Liston Range Front Light. *Photo by Bob Trapani Jr.*

of Liston Range Front Light from 1904 to 1906. Since that time, Dr. Duncan has proven to be a wonderful steward of the historic property. His unwavering dedication for preserving Delaware's last remaining wood-frame lighthouse makes him one of Delaware's finest lighthouse preservationists.

Dr. Duncan's crowning achievement as owner of the Liston Range Front Light occurred in January 2004 when the property was listed in the National Register of Historic Places, thanks to his vision and commitment to ensuring the future of the lighthouse. Aside from what he considered his duty, Dr. Duncan's motivation for initiating and following through on the National Register process was quite simple: "to inspire those that follow to maintain and preserve this maritime treasure."

The rear light serving in the Liston Range has forged its own indelible mark on Delaware lighthouse annals. First lit on May 15, 1906, Liston Range Rear Light is the state of Delaware's tallest lighthouse at 127 feet. The tower was originally built in 1877 as the rear light for the Port Penn Range, but changes to the shipping channel in 1904 forced the range to be discontinued. The United States Lighthouse Service decided to disassemble the former Port Penn Range Rear Light and re-erect the tower as the rear light for the newly established Liston Range.

Prior to the historic skeletal tower being reassembled at the site of Liston Range Rear Light, a very tall post light served as the guiding beacon. According to the 1905 *Annual Report*, the first light to show from the site was "a temporary lantern post 100 feet high, bearing a triangular lattice-work daymark, and a galvanized iron headlight lantern." This temporary light was illuminated on October 25, 1904.

When the light station was established in 1906, the United States Lighthouse Service erected only one keeper's dwelling, which was forced to house two keepers and their families. The head keeper occupied the first floor of the dwelling while the assistant keeper and his family made do with the second level of the house. This cramped environment and lack of privacy were concerns to Inspector Thomas J. Rout Jr. During his March 11, 1908 inspection of the light station, Mr. Rout noted that though the "dwelling is new and in excellent condition, accommodations should be provided for assistant keeper and his family." Unfortunately for the lightkeepers and their families, Inspector Rout's recommendations went unheeded for another five years, before finally in 1913, the U.S. Lighthouse Service constructed a second keeper's dwelling to rectify the cramped living conditions of the two families.

The classical range lens inside the rear light is of the second order and was manufactured by Barbier, Benard & Turenne, Constructeurs, of Paris, France. The beautiful Fresnel lens was installed on November 10, 1906, and

Liston Range Rear Light in the 1930s. *U.S. Coast Guard photo.*

remains in service to this day. A supplement to the United States *Coast Pilot, Atlantic Coast,* dated August 17, 1908, describes the lighthouse as showing a fixed white light 176 feet above mean high water on the Delaware River. As for the structure itself, a 1982 Historical Site Survey described the structure of Liston Range Rear Light as a black wrought-iron skeleton tower with a central stair cylinder.

Prior to electrification, the keepers of Liston Range Rear Light would illuminate the lamp at sundown and extinguish the glow at sunrise. By the mid-1930s, electric power had made its way to the light station—an advancement that ushered in the capabilities of automation—thus ending the need to have a resident keeper on site. "The lights were operated from dusk to dawn prior to a severe winter in 1936 in which the Delaware River froze over completely," said Harry Spencer Jr. "When the ice started to break up and run, it carried many of the lighted and unlighted buoys away. In light of this navigational hazard, the U.S. Lighthouse Service office in Philadelphia called dad and told him to light Liston Range Rear Light twenty-four hours a day until further notice. Well, seventy years have passed and the lighthouse is still lit twenty-four hours a day—no one ever did rescind the order."

On May 3, 2004, a new era in the history of Liston Range Rear Light was forged when the nonprofit Delaware River & Bay Lighthouse Foundation (DRBLHF) signed a thirty-year lease with the United States Coast Guard

# Liston Range Light Stations, 1906

Chief Michael Baroco, officer-in-charge, U.S. Coast Guard Aids to Navigation Team Philadelphia, cleans the second-order lens at Liston Range Rear Light. *Photo by Bob Trapani Jr.*

for the purpose of preserving the historic sentinel for future generations. The lease will enable the DRBLHF to eventually make the lighthouse accessible to the general public, which was listed in the National Register of Historic Places in 1978. The United States Coast Guard Aids to Navigation Team (ANT) in Philadelphia still maintains the light source as an aid to navigation, with the DRBLHF working to provide the necessary funding for the restoration and preservation of the lighthouse.

Chief Boatswain's Mate Michael Baroco, officer-in-charge at U.S. Coast Guard ANT Philadelphia (1999–2006) noted,

> *Having served at the USCG Aids to Navigation team responsible for Liston Range Rear Light, I have always had a particular fondness for the lighthouse. This is not just a light or a structure of wood and iron; it is a monument to the great men and women who kept these lights burning through many difficult times throughout our nation's history. I take great pride in having been able to play a role in this historic lease process. This lighthouse has allowed me to meet people I may have never known and forge friendships that I hope to keep a lifetime. Like I said, it's not just a light.*

# Chapter 19

# Harbor of Refuge Light Station
# 1908

Few lighthouses along the entire Atlantic seaboard are as exposed to the unabated fury of powerful storms as Harbor of Refuge Light Station, located a half-mile off Cape Henlopen where the Delaware Bay meets the Atlantic Ocean. In fact, the history of this rugged warrior of the sea is inseparable from the epic storms that have lashed the Delaware coastline over the last century.

A lighthouse was necessary at the site following the construction of the National Harbor of Refuge Breakwater, which commenced on May 3, 1897, and was completed December 11, 1901. The 1.5-mile-long breakwater was built along the eastern branch of the dangerous shoal called The Shears, and required 1.6 million tons of stone to construct. The breakwater project cost the United States federal government $2.5 million. The average depth of water within the Breakwater Harbor at the time of its construction was thirty-five feet and as much as seventy feet along the preferred southern end where a lighthouse was eventually erected.

The National Harbor of Refuge, which also consists of a line of stone icebreakers that extend four-tenths of a mile northwest of the breakwater, was deemed necessary to protect deeper draft vessels from the dreaded northeast winter storms. The inner Delaware Breakwater, constructed from 1829 to 1869, became insufficient as a harbor of refuge for larger commercial ships, including the warships of the United States Navy. This dilemma proved to be the driving force for the creation of the new National Harbor of Refuge Breakwater.

An interesting statement worth noting was made by the 1892 Congressional commission in charge of determining the feasibility of the project: "One of the important characteristics of a harbor of refuge is that it can be made capable of defense." The commission also informed Congress that the National Harbor of Refuge Breakwater could accommodate 1,000 vessels behind its protective stone wall.

Following completion of the breakwater, the 1902–03 edition of the *Delaware Pilot* informed its readers that the National Harbor of Refuge "might justly be called an international harbor of safety, for within its grim walls, in time of storm, lie at anchor the craft of all nations, safe from the wrath of Neptune when he seems to wish to destroy all who have invaded his domains." The account went on to state how the fame of this incredible engineering project "has spread to the uttermost confines of the globe."

The first light to mark the southern end of the breakwater and entrance into the Harbor of Refuge was established on January 1, 1902. The temporary beacon consisted of a five-day lens lantern mounted atop a thirty-foot wood frame tower. On September 16, 1903, a powerful southern storm struck the Delaware Capes and demonstrated to the breakwater engineers just how exposed and vulnerable the location was to the fury of the Atlantic.

The 1904 *Annual Report* notes that the September 1903 storm also "carried away the temporary frame light-tower, and washed from the wharf into the harbor a 2,000-pound fog-bell and striking machine which had recently been landed, and did much other minor damage. A diver was employed to search for the lost bell and striking machine, but failed to find either. The settlement of the breakwater at the site of the wharf caused by this storm was about 2 inches."

A heavy gale would once again destroy the temporary light tower at the Harbor of Refuge on November 24, 1907, but by this point great progress was made in the construction of the foundation for a lighthouse on the south end of the breakwater. Nearly a year later on November 20, 1908, the original Harbor of Refuge Lighthouse was completed and lit for the first time. The lighthouse was described as a three-story wood-frame structure painted white with lead-colored trim and a black lantern. The living quarters rested on a brown cylindrical cast-iron foundation. The cylinder was founded on a concrete block forty feet in diameter and situated fifteen feet six inches into the enrockment of the breakwater.

The light's optic consisted of a fourth-order Fresnel lens, which was illuminated by incandescent oil vapor and shined a flashing white light over the entire horizon every twelve seconds at a focal plane of fifty-two feet above sea level. Harbor of Refuge Lighthouse was

# Harbor of Refuge Light Station, 1908

Original Harbor of Refuge Lighthouse under construction in 1908. *U.S. Coast Guard photo.*

also outfitted with a first-class compressed air siren as a fog signal on October 4, 1909.

Although the original Harbor of Refuge Lighthouse was an undeniably beautiful beacon that even earned the affectionate nickname of the "Belle of the Bay," the combination of the sea's violent action and the fact that its superstructure was constructed of wood would eventually cause problems. A northeast gale on April 10–11, 1918, inflicted serious damage on Harbor of Refuge. According to lightkeeper Robert C. Taylor, the "broken lighthouse foundation shifted the big light about 2 inches on the foundation."

A February 13, 1919 report by the United States Lighthouse Service (USLHS) to Congress talked of improving the aids to navigation at the entrance to Delaware Bay. The request consisted primarily of advocating for a new lighthouse at Harbor of Refuge. The report noted, "In consequence of the continued erosion of the shore line in the vicinity of Cape Henlopen Light, Del., the early destruction of that light is anticipated, measures taken for the preservation of the shore line having proved unavailing. Every purpose now served by Cape Henlopen Light would be better served by the rebuilding of Harbor of Refuge Light to a height of about 140 feet."

The concept of rebuilding Harbor of Refuge Light as a towering conical structure never materialized, and in the interim the original wooden lighthouse continued to be assaulted by the raging Atlantic during stormy weather. On February 3–5, 1920, a fierce northeast storm hammered the Delaware coast and caused extensive damage at Harbor of Refuge. Powerful seas washed everything off the dock connected to the lighthouse, including the woodshed, fog bell, rowboat and water tanks. The worst of the storm damage was inflicted on the structure's base, which was moved another two inches off its foundation. The storms of 1918 and 1920 thus combined to move the original lighthouse a total of four inches off kilter, a fact that had to cause alarm to keepers like Robert C. Taylor.

By October 1923, the U.S. Lighthouse Service knew it wouldn't be long before the accumulative storm damage would necessitate the rebuilding of Harbor of Refuge Light. A 1924 report by Commissioner George Putnam to Congress noted that materials were collected to build a temporary tower at the site, "which is to take the place of Harbor of Refuge Light during the rebuilding of the station."

On the evening of April 12, 1926, keeper Taylor noted in his journal that "the gas light was lit [to the temporary tower] and vapor lamp [inside the lighthouse] was cut out." Taylor went on to state that contractors were building the new lighthouse. Though history has dutifully recorded the tragic loss of the nearby Cape Henlopen Lighthouse, which toppled into the sea from unchecked erosion on April 13, 1926, few people realize that the process of demolition at the original Harbor of Refuge Light began on the same day Cape Henlopen fell. The state of Delaware lost two historic lighthouses on this fateful day.

The second Harbor of Refuge Lighthouse was completed and first lit on November 15, 1926. Its fog signal, however, would not be added for another year, and it was finally reestablished on November 2, 1927. A March 1928 USLHS report noted that Harbor of Refuge was

> *adjacent to the main channel into Delaware Bay from the sea, and is now the principal aid in this locality for marine traffic originating and terminating at the Port of Philadelphia...The structure as remodeled consists of a conical tower supporting a watchroom and lantern and supported by a cylindrical pier with a flaring upper course of plates to turn the sea during rough weather. The outer shell of the pier and tower is made of cast-iron plates, the pier lined inside with reinforced concrete, and the tower proper with brick. The tower proper, in three stories, contains the keeper's quarters and the fog signal apparatus is located on the third floor. The whole structure is supported upon a heavy block of concrete lying within the breakwater.*

Despite efforts to strengthen the new Harbor of Refuge Lighthouse, the power of the sea would continue to exact a heavy toll on the site while making a lasting impression on the keepers of the light. One such storm, a northeaster, occurred April 14–16, 1929, prompting keeper Robert C. Taylor to note that "It was blowing about 78 mph; it was a pretty bad on Monday night 15<sup>th</sup>. The lighthouse shook bad. We had a job to keep the light working, the house shook so. We could not get down on the dock from Monday morning until Tuesday afternoon for the sea was washing over the top of the dock about 6 feet on the level."

Though storms continued to hammer away at the exposed location, the lighthouse was holding up to the challenge. By 1936 the USLHS *Light List* notes that Harbor of Refuge showed a flashing white light every ten seconds, with two red sectors from a fourth-order Fresnel lens that was visible fourteen nautical miles at a focal plane of seventy-two feet. The red sectors covered the hazards of Hen and Chickens Shoal to the south and Brown Shoal to the north. The light station's fog signal consisted of a first-class compressed air siren with a bell

Harbor of Refuge Lighthouse under construction in 1926. *U.S. Coast Guard photo.*

as a backup. The *Light List* also noted the height of the lighthouse from the breakwater to the top of the lantern was sixty-six feet. The structure's daymark consisted of a white conical tower and black lantern surmounting a brown cylindrical base.

The great storm of March 6–8, 1962, affected the Atlantic seaboard like few others in Delaware history, leaving behind widespread destruction in its wake up and down the mid-Atlantic region. For the keepers of Harbor of Refuge Light, the experience of enduring the tempest while surrounded by raging seas was nothing short of harrowing.

The night before the "Storm of the Century," as it was dubbed on March 5, keeper Stephen Jones remembers how the evening grew more mysterious as it wore on, noting, "The atmosphere was closing in, and yet there still seemed to be such an awful lot of sea." Jones went on to comment, "During dinner the wind began to get at us. It was not that we felt the drafts, though the venetian blinds were in constant agitation. It was more that we seem to have been sought out by invisible currents and isolated in unfocused eddies of irritation."

During the middle of the night the tempest's fury increased dramatically, with powerful waves buffeting the tower and causing the furniture to shudder and eventually become rearranged. At one point a rogue wave shattered a second-story window, some forty feet above the water. Later the remnants of another wave found its way inside a first-floor window, which caused the keeper's lone communication with the outside world—the radio—to explode. "While there certainly was a lot going on inside the tower, there seemed to be a fair amount going on outside as well, and a good amount of the outside was trying to happen inside," said lightkeeper Jones.

Meanwhile, the engine room in the tower's basement was filled with six inches of water as the frightening volume of the Atlantic rose sufficiently over the massive breakwater to establish its realm inside the lighthouse under full assault by the storm. With real concerns about whether the lighthouse could hold up under the incredible punishment inflicted upon it, the keepers anxiously went about their work to keep the station from falling into total disarray. Trips to the light's lantern only compounded their dire situation as the keepers felt the full sway of the tower at its pinnacle in the face of the maelstrom.

The ominous gray skies and raging Atlantic Ocean combined to conceal the time of day, prompting keeper Jones to say, "Morning did not come. Time did pass, measured by dripping, erased by swaying." Jones continued, "From the east, I saw out into such a mass of water as I'd not thought possible." At the height of the northeast tempest, canned

Harbor of Refuge Lighthouse in the late 1950s. *Lewes Historical Society.*

goods were falling off the pantry shelves and later the sentinel lost power to all of its interior lights, forcing the keepers to work feverishly to start the generators and restore light throughout the tower.

Nearly forty years to the exact date of the great March northeaster, on March 9, 2002, former lightkeeper Stephen Jones returned to Harbor of Refuge Light for the first time with members of the Delaware River & Bay Lighthouse Foundation. During his return, Jones recounted his experience of being aboard the lighthouse during this terrifying storm.

He returned again to Harbor of Refuge in June 2004 and participated as a volunteer on five lighthouse tours, delighting tour patrons with his firsthand accounts of the March 1962 storm. Visitors to the lighthouse were stunned to hear Jones say, "We didn't see the breakwater for three days. The stone wall was completely underwater." When asked if he and his fellow lightkeepers had any idea of the magnitude of the storm at the time, Jones replied, "No. It wasn't like there was someone telling us, 'this is the storm of the century.' It took forty years to pass for us to learn of that distinction."

Though the last Coast Guard keepers were removed in December 1973 following the automation of the light station, Harbor of Refuge received new modern-day "keepers" when the nonprofit Delaware River & Bay Lighthouse Foundation (DRBLHF) based in Lewes signed a twenty-year historic lease with the United States Coast Guard for Harbor of Refuge Light on April 1, 2002. Senior Chief Dennis Dever, officer-in-charge at the time of U.S. Coast Guard Aids to Navigation Team Cape May, New Jersey, noted, "The lease on Harbor of Refuge Light is a great thing in that the DRBLHF can make positive restoration progress of the historic site. The Coast Guard today simply could not do this on our own with such limited resources. The DRBLHF, like other organizations that truly want to preserve a lighthouse, is stepping up to the plate and making it happen."

The DRBLHF's two vice-presidents—Michael DiPaolo and Greg Ositko—captured the significance of the lease signing with DiPaolo noting, "We cannot shrink from this project. It is a large pursuit, probably the single largest historic preservation project undertaken in the state of Delaware." Ositko echoed DiPaolo's sentiments: "This historic event presents the most fervent, challenging and steadfast community project of a nature and magnitude, which will have no end—only boundless educational and preservation opportunities for generations to come."

On September 30, 2004, the U.S. Department of the Interior transferred ownership of Harbor of Refuge Light to the Delaware

Former Harbor of Refuge Lighthouse keeper Stephen Jones. *Photo by Bob Trapani Jr.*

River & Bay Lighthouse Foundation during a historic lighthouse ceremony held at the Cape May–Lewes Ferry's terminal in Lewes. The DRBLHF acquired the lighthouse through the National Historic Lighthouse Preservation Act. Dan Smith of the National Park Service, who represented U.S. Department of the Interior Secretary Gale Norton, announced to the audience during the ceremony, "This is a good day for Delaware and for lighthouses."

# Chapter 20

# Bellevue Range Light Stations
## 1909

The Bellevue Range, which is located between the towns of Edgemoor and Claymont, Delaware, was first lit on March 15, 1909. The establishment of the Bellevue Range adjacent to the nearby Christiana Lighthouse forced the decommissioning of the old 1835 lighthouse, which was originally built to mark the entrance to the Christiana River.

The historic Bellevue Range Front Light was apparently short-lived, and the passage of time refuses to reveal much more than scant details about the structure and its length of service. The 1909 *Annual Report* notes that the front light was "a fixed white reflector, lighting during periods of 2 seconds, separated by eclipses of 1 second's duration." The optic was described as a locomotive-type headlight lamp, with a candlepower of 2,500 that was exhibited from a height of thirty-five feet above high water.

As for the lighthouse structure itself, it consisted of a one-story wood-frame building painted white with lead-colored trimmings, green blinds and a brown square lantern that rose up from the center of the dwelling. The structure was rather small and confining with only three rooms, including the watchroom. The keeper procured the station's drinking water via a 575-gallon cedar tank, which collected water from the downspouts and was located in the hallway on the first floor, further cramping the interior of the beacon.

A March 8, 1909 inspection report notes the now-obscure light station was located on a timber bulkhead about one-half mile below the Edgemoor Iron Works. The Edgemoor Bulkhead extended into the water some 4,200 feet, which was far enough out in the Delaware River for a lighthouse tender to land alongside to resupply the lighthouse.

The original Bellevue Range Front Light was listed as being thirty-four feet tall from its base to the vent, with a focal plane of thirty-five feet. According to the inspection report, the "lantern was of the fourth order, cylindrical in shape at its base, and polygonal above the sill. Balustrade is of wrought iron; gallery is of wood covered with tin." Though the lighthouse was a compact building, it was still equipped with a call bell system that was installed in the watchroom and connected with the clockwork. The bell itself was located on the wall of the first floor hall.

The original optic was a locomotion headlight reflector thirteen by twenty-two inches in size. The light's occulting characteristic was accomplished by a brass shade lifted and dropped around the chimney of the optic by clockwork. The fifth-order locomotion headlight lamp and reflector were supported on a wooden cupboard. In addition to the lighthouse, the station was also equipped with a five-by-ten-foot wooden oil house, which was located about twenty-eight feet south of the lighthouse. By 1912 acetylene replaced the oil wick as the beacon's illumination source.

A 1923 *Report of the Commissioner of Lighthouses* would spell eventual doom for the original lighthouse through an appropriation request of $8,000 to rebuild the station. According to the report, "The present light is in a wooden structure on the wooden pile bulkhead known as Edgemoor Bulkhead. The structure and its foundation are decayed to such an extent as to render the necessity for a complete replacement urgent. It is proposed to construct a submarine concrete foundation with ice breaker back of bulkhead and erect thereon a 31-foot standard structural steel tower equipped with L-350 range gas lantern."

Subsequent appropriation requests were made each year thereafter until Congress finally funded the construction of a new Bellevue Range Front Light in 1929. The new skeleton tower was simple in design, brown in color and bore a slatted wood daymark.

Unlike the front light, the Bellevue Range Rear Light not only has survived the ravages of time, but also has the unique distinction of being the only Delaware lighthouse to have changed locations without ever being moved. When the skeleton sentinel was established in 1909, the tower stood approximately one hundred yards offshore in shallow water from the Delaware River's western bank and about one thousand feet north of the entrance to the Christiana River. The keepers accessed the water-locked tower by a wooden walkway that spanned the tidal waters and mudflats.

Over the ensuing years, dredge and fill material was deposited along the western bank that was slowly but surely extending out to the lighthouse and eventually overtaking it by two thousand feet. The extension of the man-made shoreline effectively relocated Bellevue Range Rear Light from the Delaware River into the Christiana River without moving it. The land that borders the northern side of Bellevue Range Rear Light later became a landfill for Wilmington and the surrounding Delaware region, which remains active to this day.

The black pyramidal skeleton lighthouse was built to a height of 104 feet, standing about 1.1 miles behind the range front light. At high tide the tower was surrounded by nearly 5 feet of water but when the tide receded the lighthouse stood on a mud flat about 1.5 feet above mean low water. The structure was built of cast and wrought iron and situated on nine concrete piers. A brick oil house was located 950 feet from the tower on shore near the keeper's dwelling.

The lighthouse was originally equipped with a fourth-order range lens that showed a fixed white light from a 100-foot focal plane. An inspection report dated February 16, 1910, notes that the light's characteristic was a flashing white light every 2½ seconds with incandescent oil vapor serving as the illuminant source. The lens itself revolved and consisted of eight panels. The revolving process was powered by fourth-order clockworks that required winding every 7.5 hours. A bell system connected to clockwork was replaced in 1910 by a telephone system to the dwelling that allowed the keeper to call for assistance.

According to the 1910 inspection report, the head keeper's dwelling consisted of a white brick building with lead-colored trimming, green shutters and a slate roof, located about 980 feet northwest of the tower. Other outbuildings included a frame barn, brick oil house, privy, frame tank house, poultry house and small storehouse. The assistant keeper's house was described as concrete, white in color, with wooden framing and floors and located about one thousand feet northwest of the tower.

For a period of time, the keepers at Bellevue Range Rear Light also kept the nearby Christiana North Jetty Light and may have been assigned the duties of tending the front light of the Bellevue Range once the keeper at that light was removed. The first hint of the range rear light being capable of sustaining an automated light came in 1919 when an acetylene light replaced the incandescent oil vapor. Despite the upgrade in illumination technology, a keeper was maintained at the light station until about 1934 when the lighthouse was made fully automated.

The historic Bellevue Range Rear Light is no longer operational, having been discontinued on December 14, 2000, due to the height of the landfill obscuring the beacon's light despite the structure's 104-foot stature. Though the landfill was rising for years, no one realized just how close the man-made hill was to eclipsing the rear light until the late 1990s when a refuse truck happened to block the range line at the exact moment the pilot of a down-

# Bellevue Range Light Stations, 1909

Bellevue Range Rear Light in 1909. *U.S. Coast Guard photo.*

Bellevue Range Rear Light. *Photo by Bob Trapani Jr.*

bound ship on the Delaware was observing the light. This dilemma caused the U.S. Coast Guard to establish a modern skeleton tower atop the landfill in place of the old beacon. The new Bellevue Range Rear Light is now only 1,085 yards behind the front light, versus the historic structure, which stands 2,240 yards back.

# Chapter 21

## Marcus Hook Range Rear Light Station

### 1920

Delaware's northernmost lighthouse is neither the state's oldest nor the tallest, but it does have a few distinctions that no other sentinel on the Delaware River and Bay—or in one case, the entire Atlantic seaboard—possesses. Even though the lighthouse rises 105 feet above the residential community of Gordon Heights between Edgemoor and Bellefonte, Delaware, that fact alone isn't distinctly noteworthy. What makes Marcus Hook Range Rear Light such an imposing presence along the East Coast is the height that its light is seen above sea level.

When you factor in that the light is perched on a large hill that overlooks the Delaware River, it is the combination of the height of the lighthouse tower and the hill itself that makes it special in American lighthouse history. The October 6, 1949 edition of the *Reno (Nevada) Evening Gazette* cites this distinction as "Highest Lighthouse…The rear range light of Marcus Hook on the Delaware River, 278 feet above the level of the sea, is the highest light on the Atlantic coast of the continental United States."

Another distinction the Marcus Hook Range possesses—this one being a "little closer to home"—is that it was the last manned pair of range lights built along the Delaware River and Bay when officially completed in 1920. Over a forty-year period that began in the mid-1870s, the U.S. Lighthouse Service put forth a constant effort to work with pilots, ship owners and other maritime stakeholders to petition

# Marcus Hook Range Rear Light Station, 1920

Marcus Hook Range Rear Light. *Photo by Ann-Marie Trapani.*

The Fresnel range lens at Marcus Hook Range Rear Light. *Courtesy of the Delaware State Historic Preservation Office.*

Congress for appropriations to improve the aids to navigation system on the Delaware River. Due to dangerous rocky ledges and shoals, as well as derelict wrecks and tight turns on the Delaware River, the presence of range lights was vital to safeguarding ships heading for the ports of Philadelphia, Wilmington and Camden.

In 1915 the Lighthouse Service erected temporary light towers at both Marcus Hook Range Front Light and Marcus Hook Range Rear Light until the permanent structures could be completed. The 1919 *Report of the Commissioner of Lighthouses* describes the permanent front light upon completion that year as consisting "of a concrete block on a pile foundation at low-water mark, supporting a 72-foot structural-steel tower, from which is shown a flashing, automatic, acetylene light."

The Marcus Hook Range Rear Light, standing 1⅔ miles to the rear of the range front light, was of a completely different design. Built of reinforced concrete, the lighthouse is a square tower with buttressed corners surmounted by a watchroom and lantern room at the pinnacle of the massive structure. The interior of the tower, though unimaginative architecturally, contains some noteworthy components as well. A metal staircase with landings every twenty-five feet leads to a spacious watchroom originally built as a chart and radio room. The lantern room is accessed directly above the watchroom via a metal ladder. Outside the lantern room is a four-foot-wide concrete balcony.

According to the light's National Register of Historic Places nomination form, "The tower below the gallery was poured in nine sections. Each section, other than the topmost, has one window so that there are two openings on each side of the tower, with the space varying from side to side." The light station also contains a former brick lightkeeper's dwelling and one outbuilding that served such different functions as an oil shed, garage and storage area. When the lighthouse was completed in 1920, a fixed white light was shown from a fourth-order range lens illuminated by incandescent oil vapor. The original fourth-order range lens was removed from the lighthouse in the early 1980s and is now on display at the Independence Seaport Museum in Philadelphia.

The General Services Administration listed Marcus Hook Range Rear Light as surplus government property on March 9, 2005, offering ownership of the light station to eligible government agencies as well as interested nonprofit organizations through the National Historic Lighthouse Preservation Act application process, administered by the National Park Service. Though the lighthouse will have new caretakers in time, the light source in Marcus Hook Range Rear Light will remain an active guide to shipping on the Delaware River and continue to be maintained by USCG Aids to Navigation Team Philadelphia.

# Chapter 22

## Delaware Lighthouse Preservation

The state of Delaware has a proud and long-standing heritage when it comes to lighthouses. From colonial times through the present day, the First State's guardians of the sea have continued to protect mariners seeking the waters of the Delaware Bay and River, but they also shine a brilliant symbolic light on the history, culture and future growth of Delaware. Sadly, the elements, erosion, neglect, vandalism and occasional indifference have exacted a heavy toll on Delaware's historic lighthouses.

In all, the federal government established twenty-seven different light stations along Delaware's coastline, starting with the legendary Cape Henlopen Lighthouse in 1767. The last historic lighthouse to be built in Delaware is the present-day Harbor of Refuge Lighthouse, which was constructed in 1926—the same year Cape Henlopen Light toppled into the Atlantic Ocean. Today, only nine of the twenty-seven historic light stations remain, and even some of these are endangered.

In an effort to help save the First State's lighthouse heritage and educate the public on the irreplaceable value of these benevolent beacons, author Bob Trapani Jr. and Dan McFadden cofounded the nonprofit Delaware River & Bay Lighthouse Foundation (DRBLHF) on February 7, 1999. The mission of the organization was firmly rooted in active participation for the preservation of Delaware's remaining lighthouses—a commitment that was demonstrated through the DRBLHF's efforts to eventually obtain stewardship responsibilities for three of Delaware's nine present-day lighthouses.

The Delaware River & Bay Lighthouse Foundation obtained its first lighthouse when the organization signed a twenty-year lease with the United States Coast Guard for Harbor of Refuge Light on April 1, 2002.

Volunteers began working at the lighthouse on a monthly basis in August 2002 and have continued to perform a variety of maintenance tasks at the site, including rebuilding the wooden landing decks at the light four times during 2003 because of storm damage. The DRBLHF made mid-Atlantic lighthouse history when it became the first organization to open an offshore lighthouse to the general public for tours on June 21, 2003. The following year over one thousand people were able to journey out to visit Harbor of Refuge Light through DRBLHF educational tours and programs.

The stalwart Harbor of Refuge would make history again in fall 2004 when it became the first Delaware lighthouse to be transferred by the U.S. Department of the Interior to a nonprofit (DRBLHF) through the National Historic Lighthouse Preservation Act on September 30, 2004.

The September 28–30, 2004 edition of the *Cape Gazette* in Lewes, Delaware, noted in the newspaper's editorial section that "such transfers aren't approved haphazardly. Organizations receiving these historic structures go through extensive screening to ensure worthiness. It comes as no surprise to those who have watched the determined and professional work of the DRBLHF over the past several years that it passed muster in the eyes of the Department of the Interior. Bob Trapani and his crew of dedicated volunteers have invested hundreds of hours of hard labor and expertise to retard the deterioration of the Harbor of Refuge Lighthouse."

The editorial went on to state, "They have also cleaned up the interior of the historic structure and given it life by removing plywood covers from its windows so that we can once again look into its soul and see colors of sunrises and sunsets reflecting from its glass. Their work has enabled dozens of groups to make visits to the outer wall, tour the lighthouse, and gain an incomparable feel for the historic importance of the massive stone breakwater and beacon on the eastern edge of our American continent."

Delaware Public Archives later commemorated the historical importance of the lighthouse, breakwater and transfer of ownership from the federal government to the DRBLHF by partnering with the nonprofit to dedicate a bronze historic marker at the offshore site on November 27, 2004. The Harbor of Refuge Lighthouse historic marker has the distinction of being the first of its kind dedicated at a Delaware offshore location.

The second lighthouse to come under the care of the DRBLHF was the land-based Liston Range Rear Light, located near Port Penn. The organization signed a thirty-year historic lease with the United States Coast Guard on May 3, 2004. The lease included preservation responsibilities for both the 1877 tower and the adjacent enamel brick oil house. Members of the Chesapeake Chapter of the United States Lighthouse Society

U.S. Coast Guard and DRBLHF sign historic lease on May 3, 2004. *Back row, left to right:* Greg Ositko, Judith Roales, Harry Spencer Jr. and Tom Craft. *Front row, left to right:* Michelle Miller Frieden, Bob Trapani and Chief Michael Baroco. *Photo by Ann-Marie Trapani.*

participated in the first public tour of Liston Range Rear Light when the enthusiastic group climbed 177 stairs to the top of Delaware's tallest sentinel on April 24, 2005.

The offshore Delaware Breakwater East End Light became the third lighthouse to come under the stewardship of the DRBLHF through a groundbreaking formal operating agreement with the Delaware River & Bay Authority (DRBA). Following approval from the National Park Service and the Delaware State Historic Preservation Office, the DRBLHF and DRBA officially announced the partnership to the general public on September 30, 2004. This unique partnership will enable the DRBLHF and DRBA to work together on the preservation and educational interpretation of the Delaware Breakwater East End Lighthouse. The first public tour of the lighthouse occurred on May 20, 2006.

As is the case with all lighthouse restoration projects, education is a vital component to ensuring the long-term care of each beacon. Without an understanding and appreciation for the importance of Delaware's historic lighthouses, cultivating a sustainable interest within the community for their preservation would be a near impossible task, especially for the offshore lights.

A major education effort designed to raise greater awareness for offshore lighthouses like Delaware Breakwater East End and Harbor of Refuge occurred in 2004 when the DRBLHF, DRBA and Delaware Public Archives collaborated on an exciting initiative to install historic markers for both lighthouses at the Lewes terminal of the Cape May–Lewes Ferry.

The historic markers were sponsored by State Senator Gary Simpson and State Representative Joseph Booth of the Delaware General Assembly through the Delaware Public Archives program under the leadership of Russ McCabe. The establishment of the informative historic markers along the Lewes Ferry terminal will now help educate the thousands of people who pass through the terminal each year.

The markers were dedicated during the same historic ceremony in which the DRBLHF received ownership of Harbor of Refuge Light from the U.S. Department of the Interior and the public announcement of the DRBLHF/DRBA partnership of the Delaware Breakwater East End Light on September 30, 2004. The four separate ceremonies that occurred during this unprecedented September event at the Lewes Ferry terminal constituted the most historic moment in the First State's modern lighthouse history.

Like all nonprofit lighthouse preservation organizations, the Delaware River & Bay Lighthouse Foundation cannot help save the First State's lighthouse heritage without the ongoing financial and volunteer support from

*Left to right*: City of Lewes Mayor James Ford, James Johnson, Senator Thomas R. Carper, Bob Trapani and John Sarro visit Delaware Breakwater East End Light on September 10, 2004, to discuss the beacon's present and future. *Photo by Ann-Marie Trapani.*

# Delaware Lighthouse Preservation

Delaware Breakwater East End Light historic marker dedication on September 30, 2004. *Left to right*: James Johnson, Delaware Senator Gary Simpson, Bob Trapani, Russ McCabe, Delaware Representative Joseph Booth, Daniel Griffith and William Lowe III. *Photo by Ann-Marie Trapani.*

the general public. Though the DRBLHF has forged some wonderful new chapters in lighthouse history to date, the work to save the state's lighthouses is a journey that has no end. If you admire and cherish Delaware's guiding beacons, consider becoming involved today with the DRBLHF and become a keeper of our lights!

To learn more about the efforts of the Delaware River & Bay Lighthouse Foundation, contact:

*Delaware River & Bay Lighthouse Foundation*
*PO Box 708*
*Lewes, DE 19958*
*302.644.7046*
*www.delawarebaylights.org*

LV 118 / Lightship *Overfalls*. Photo by Bob Trapani Jr.

Though not a lighthouse in the traditional terms, lightship LV 118 nonetheless once served as a "floating lighthouse" and thus deserves rightful mention when reviewing the history of Delaware's guiding lights. Despite the fact that this vessel never served on a Delaware lightship station (instead serving at Cornfield Point, Connecticut; Cross Rip, Massachusetts; and Boston, Massachusetts stations from 1938 to 1970), the bright red ship bears the name *Overfalls* in honor of the lightship station that was located at the junction of the Delaware Bay and Atlantic Ocean.

LV 118 was the last lightship built by the United States Lighthouse Service in 1938 and today is one of only seventeen surviving lightships nationwide. The lightship, located prominently along the Lewes Canal, is cared for and being restored by the energetic nonprofit Overfalls Maritime Museum Foundation (OMMF).

The lightship was originally obtained by the Lewes Historical Society (LHS) from the U.S. Coast Guard in 1972. During 1999 a group of individuals in Lewes became interested in making the *Overfalls* lightship a full-time preservation project. Though the LV 118 would remain a part of the LHS for two more years, the hardy volunteers seeking to restore the vessel were rewarded for their passionate interest when the historical society transferred ownership of the lightship to the newly formed Overfalls Maritime Museum Foundation on December 7, 2001.

Since that time, the OMMF has worked tirelessly to restore the ship's interior and exterior, while seeking a long-term solution for the ship's deteriorating hull, which is stuck in about seven to ten feet of muck and mire along the Lewes Canal. A proud lightship moment occurred on October 3, 2003, as OMMF chair Gary Stabley, vice-chair Elaine Simmerman, Delaware State Senator Gary Simpson, Mayor James Ford of Lewes and Russ McCabe of Delaware Public Archives, unveiled and dedicated a bronze historical marker at the site to commemorate the importance of the lightship to the First State.

To learn more about the exciting efforts to save LV 118 for future generations, contact:

*Overfalls Maritime Museum Foundation*
*PO Box 413*
*Lewes, DE 19958*
*302.644.8050*
*www.overfalls.org*

# Delaware Lighthouse Preservation

Lighthouse preservation isn't simply about the structures, but the artifacts and memories of the men, women and children who helped keep the lights shining bright along Delaware's coastline as well. No one is more dedicated to preserving the human interest aspect of Delaware's proud lighthouse heritage than the Lewes Historical Society (LHS).

Over the past forty-plus years, the LHS has developed a highly respected reputation within the state of Delaware as a trusted repository for a wealth of priceless history, including the lighthouses of the Delaware River and Bay. The lighthouse artifact of greatest pride to the LHS is the gorgeous fourth-order Fresnel lens from Fourteen Foot Bank Lighthouse, Delaware Bay. Lewes Historical Society executive director Michael DiPaolo notes the importance of the lens as an educational exhibit, stating, "The lens is the centerpiece of one of our galleries—literally and figuratively. We are working on plans to gradually integrate interactive experiences for visitors to learn more about not only how lighthouses work, but to gain a better appreciation for the lights of Delaware Bay and the men and women who served at them."

To learn more about this fine collection of lighthouse artifacts and history, contact:

*Lewes Historical Society*
*110 Shipcarpenter St.*
*Lewes, DE 19958*
*302.645.7670*
*www.historiclewes.org*

The American Lighthouse Foundation (ALF), a national leader in lighthouse preservation, is lending support to the effort to save Delaware's lighthouse heritage. In addition to applying for ownership of Fourteen Foot Bank Lighthouse through the National Historic Lighthouse Preservation Act at the end of 2005, the organization is helping advocate for the repair of the National Harbor of Refuge Breakwater.

Over the past thirty years, Father Time and powerful storm waves have exacted a heavy toll on the south end of the massive 1.5-mile-long stone breakwater. The alarming deterioration and undermining of the stone wall that has occurred over the last three decades now threatens to topple the Harbor of Refuge Lighthouse into the sea. In an effort to prevent the tragic loss of this stalwart sentinel, the American Lighthouse Foundation is joining with the

Michael DiPaolo, Lewes Historical Society executive director, stands next the Fourteen Foot Bank Lighthouse Fresnel lens exhibit located inside the Cannonball Museum. *Photo by Bob Trapani Jr.*

Delaware River & Bay Lighthouse Foundation and other First State maritime and community stakeholders to advocate for the breakwater's repair.

ALF submitted a $1.5 federal appropriation to Congress through United States Senator Thomas R. Carper in January 2006 on behalf of the National Harbor of Refuge Breakwater. The appropriation request would provide the Army Corps of Engineers with the funds necessary to enact stabilization repairs to the breakwater and save Harbor of Refuge Lighthouse in the process. The funding request was a direct result of the Army Corps of Engineers findings during a side-scan survey performed in December 2005.

To learn more about the efforts of the American Lighthouse Foundation, contact:

*American Lighthouse Foundation*
*PO Box 889*
*Wells, ME 04090*
*207.646.0245*
*www.lighthousefoundation.org*

# Delaware Lighthouse Preservation

Harbor of Refuge Light is routinely pounded by the Atlantic Ocean. *Photo by Herb Von Goerres.*

Senior Chief Dennis Dever, officer-in-charge, U.S. Coast Guard Aids to Navigation Team Cape May, New Jersey (2000-04). *Photo by Bob Trapani Jr.*

The tragic losses of lighthouses like Cape Henlopen, Port Mahon and Mispillion are vivid examples to the fact that time and the elements do not afford us a second chance when it comes to rising up and seizing the moment in lighthouse preservation. Our country will not build these mighty edifices again. With each loss of these historic sites, a major piece of Delaware itself is lost forever. Even now, the future of some of Delaware's remaining nine lighthouses is murky. It is up to you and I to do something about saving these guardians of the First State before another historic catastrophe is permitted to occur. The passion and determination of just a few people can make all the difference in the world—and you can be that person to help save Delaware's lighthouse heritage!

# Delaware Lighthouse Preservation

Retired United States Coast Guard Master Chief Dennis E. Dever and former lightkeeper at the historic Boston Light Station in Massachusetts eloquently reflects upon and sums up the importance of lighthouse preservation:

> *Taking care of lighthouses is a great thing in that they are a timeless constant in the history of our country and in our local areas. As people, styles and events come and go—the lighthouse remains. A lighthouse is the first thing mariners see approaching land and the last thing they watch departing to sea. A lighthouse is always in the background tolerating its surroundings. Interest in preservation ensures the lighthouse remains stable while the world continues to evolve.*

# Selected Bibliography

Barnes, Robert C., and Judith M. Pfeiffer. *Press, Politics, and Perseverance*. New Castle, DE: Oak Knoll Press and Pine Tree Books, 1999.

Beach, John W. *Cape Henlopen Lighthouse and Delaware Breakwater*. Dover, DE: Dover Litho Printing Company, 1970.

*Blunt's American Coast Pilot*.

Brittingham, Hazel D. *Lantern on Lewes: Where the Past is Present*. Lewes, DE: Lewestown Publishers, 1998.

*Cape Gazette*.

Clunies, Sandy. "The Christy Mystery." *Chesapeake Lights*. Winter 2004.

Delaware River & Bay Lighthouse Foundation. *The Bay Pilot*. Lewes, DE.

Evans, Douglas J. "The History of Cape Henlopen Lighthouse, 1764–1926." Senior thesis, University of Delaware, May 17, 1958.

Gowdy, Jim, and Kim Ruth. *Guiding Lights of the Delaware River & Bay*. Egg Harbor City, NJ: Laureate Press, 1999.

Jones, Stephen. *Harbor of Refuge*. Hanover, NH: University Press of New England, 2000.

# *Selected Bibliography*

Kyle, Mary Pat. *Fenwick Island: Ice Age to Jet Age*. Fenwick Island, DE, 1995.

*Lighthouse Digest*.

Lynch-Morris, Dorothy. Excerpts of oral histories from her childhood at Port Mahon Lighthouse, courtesy of Penny Czerwinski (unpublished).

Philadelphia Maritime Exchange. *Eighty-eight Nautical Miles on the Delaware*. Philadelphia: George S. Harris & Sons, 1950.

————. *Hand Book of the Lower Delaware River*. Philadelphia: George S. Harris & Sons, 1895.

Putnam, George R. *Lighthouses and Lightships of the United States*. Boston: Houghton Mifflin, 1933.

Ramsey, Kelvin, and Marijke J. Reilly. "The Hurricane of October 21–24, 1878." Delaware Geological Survey No. 22, Newark: University of Delaware, 2002.

Taylor, Robert C. Excerpts from personal journal penned during his tenure as keeper at Harbor of Refuge Lighthouse. Courtesy of Sherry Mitchell (unpublished).

Trapani, Bob, Jr. *Lighthouses of New Jersey and Delaware: History, Mystery, Legend and Lore*. Elkton, MD: Myst and Lace Publishers, 2005.

United States Coast Guard *Light List*.

United States *Coast Pilot*.

United States Lighthouse Service. *Annual Reports* (various years).

————. *Light List*.

# About the Author

ob Trapani Jr. was born in Pottstown, Pennsylvania, and now resides in Wells, Maine, with his wife, Ann-Marie, and their three children Nina, Katrina and Dominic.

Bob serves as the executive director for the American Lighthouse Foundation (ALF), a national lighthouse preservation organization headquartered in Wells, Maine. ALF is the steward of twenty-two historic lighthouses throughout New England and owns the Museum of Lighthouse History, also located in Wells.

Prior to this Bob served as the president (1999–2005) for the Delaware River & Bay Lighthouse Foundation (DRBLHF) in Lewes, Delaware, which he co-founded in 1999. Under his leadership the DRBLHF secured ownership of Harbor of Refuge Lighthouse from the Department of the Interior through the National Historic Lighthouse Preservation Act, obtained a long-term lease of Liston Range Rear Light from the U.S. Coast Guard and forged a groundbreaking partnership with the Delaware River & Bay Authority for the preservation of Delaware Breakwater East End Light.

*About the Author*

In addition, Bob served four years—from 2000 to 2004—as the executive director of the Delaware Seashore Preservation Foundation, caretakers of the historic 1876 Indian River Life-Saving Station Museum, located in Rehoboth Beach, Delaware. During his tenure at the lifesaving station, Bob authored his first book *Journey Along the Sands: A History of the Indian River Life-Saving Station* in 2002.

He also enjoys volunteering his time to the United States Coast Guard as an auxiliarist, having spent five years with the USCG Aids to Navigation Team Cape May, New Jersey (2000–2005). He now works with Coast Guard aids to navigation teams in Maine. Bob was awarded the prestigious U.S. Coast Guard Auxiliary Meritorious Service Award for his contributions to the field of aids to navigation from 2001 through 2003.

Bob is a contributing writer for *Lighthouse Digest* magazine and *Wreck & Rescue*, a publication of the United States Life-Saving Service Heritage Association. He also has authored *Lighthouses of New Jersey and Delaware: History, Mystery, Legend & Lore* (2005) and *Lighthouses of Maryland and Virginia: History, Mystery, Legend & Lore* (2006).